# A EUROPEAN ODYSSEY

## HOW A BOXER'S DAUGHTER FOUND GRACE

### BAILEY ALEXANDER

*For Muv*

# PROLOGUE

## Death and Prayer in Positano

~

P rior to my brother's death I booked a ten-day
cooking trip in Positano. Instead of meeting up with
my husband somewhere on the continent I decided
to extend it and take Muv to Europe for a month. I needed to
put a pause in the family drama. I needed to separate my
mother from the shock and humiliation of her son's memorial service. I thought I could take her away from death and
give her a vacation from grief. We spent ten days in Italy
before driving up to Paris, then two days in London. It was
time well spent together; our mother-daughter dynamic
shifted and we became best of friends.

The first two weeks we stayed at a favorite hotel called
Villa Franca hanging off a cliff overlooking the Mediterranean on the Amalfi Coast. Each morning I, along with
eight fellow food enthusiasts, eagerly took notes at the
home of our teacher, Diana Folonari. Her villa was within

walking distance from the hotel. It also overlooked the sea and we couldn't believe our good fortune. After two hours of cutting vegetables and learning the art of 'Slow Food' we drank white wine and proceeded to eat our morning lesson for lunch.

Then I headed down to the beach to find Muv. She was easy to locate because she often ate at the same place. I always found her enjoying her second or third cup of American black coffee while Italian waiters happily fawned over her. I doubt many tourists acted as grateful as Muv, indulging in a plate of pasta every day, sometimes both at lunch and dinner. After a lifetime of a relatively strict diet it was time to let it go. Everything was perfect and if it wasn't, she didn't complain because she rarely did.

We visited Pompeii and after our history lesson we silently concluded we'd had enough of death. Positano provided a kinder solution with heavy sun to give us cover. Our itinerary didn't deviate much because we were content to roam aimlessly around town, checking out the art and life on display. We bought books from local artists and lit candles in the churches.

Italy felt like a balm and each time we entered a church we took back our own interpretation of religion. Muv never lit a candle; sometimes there were dozens already flickering. In public she wore her religion as lightly as Italians often do in private. She watched me light candles, then she'd study the interiors, imbibing the glamorous traditions, replacing everything the evangelicals had managed to scrape out of the experience. The smells along with all the elegant pomp and ceremony fell back in place. During Blaine's illness I knew Muv often went to a large gothic Catholic Church on Capitol Hill.

Walking out of the dark ambiance into the bright Italian

sun, Muv would casually say, "Maybe I should convert, they do it so well."

The majority of our time was spent walking up and down steps and gawking at the view. Each day ended the same way: after dinner we came back to the hotel, our refuge, to loiter over a glass of wine or a cup of coffee at the bar. It was a pleasure to retire to our voluminous bedroom with its high ceilings and whimsical floor covered in blue and yellow ceramic times. There were two double twin beds and a charming spacious balcony overlooking the bluest sea we'd ever seen.

No matter where she was, whether in Seattle, San Francisco, or Positano, Muv woke up early to allow plenty of time to properly put on her face and get dressed. It was same process in reverse before getting into bed. She never deviated from this routine. When I was still small enough to sit on the bathroom counter with my feet in the sink, I found it hypnotic to watch her. We both studied her image in the mirror as she applied her make up. If her eyes caught mine they'd close slightly in her attempt to smile while putting on her lipstick. Even the small act of putting on lipstick seemed to have a purpose. I think her elaborate routine was a form of meditation in response to having five kids and multiple activities throughout the day. My parents spent a lifetime driving us from one event to the next. Once upon a time we must have been happy, of this I was convinced.

Never considered beautiful in the classical sense, my mother was handsome and took care to keep everything that way for as long as possible. The first task was her teeth. Flossing was followed by a tiny rubber tool used to massage in between each tooth. Seated on the edge of the bathtub, lost in thought, one hand resting on her lap until it was time for the final brush. She stood up in front of the mirror, her three fingers applying Pond's Cold Cream with specific circular motions covering first her forehead as she pushed back her grey bangs, then face and neck. Sometimes her mouth would move as if repeating a piece of recent conversation. When she was satisfied with a personal edit she might say it out loud.

I felt like a kid again watching her swipe a tissue from the Kleenex box and glide by my bed onto the terrace. She stopped and surveyed the scene, each time like it was the first. Time was still on her side; I doubt she even knew how to waste it. My routine was a relatively quick affair and I was in bed, sitting up against the pillows reading a short story by David Sedaris out loud. The one about his brother who keeps sticking his tongue into the light socket in the classroom.

I have trouble finishing the story because I'm laughing so hard. "Can you believe that?" I gasp.

Muv responds straight away as if wanting to throw me the one thought on her mind. With a playful but direct gaze she emphasized each word, "Oh yes, you all had your own little quirks."

I stopped laughing because she left a cloud of seriousness in her wake. She wanted lots of kids and got them. She enjoyed the noise, the activity, the distractions as long as she could carve out her own time, which she did. I closed the book and followed her out onto the terrace. The sun had set but there was plenty of light in the sky. I watched her figure motionless in front of the wrought iron balcony. Her hands on the railing, her palms relaxed, facing the sky, perhaps in prayer. My bed was next to the terrace, her profile in full view. I knew her thoughts were filled with her son. He's young and alive, and we're all full of quirks, and Muv is perfectly serene.

# 1

## HOW OLD ARE YOU DARLING?

### 1999

∽

I have my mother to thank for losing my mind. She pushed the first domino that fell into a series, inspiring me to leave all that security in Seattle, and sail across the Atlantic with my husband and two small dogs. Her confession created the kind of upheaval that forced me to look at myself, my society, and my country in a completely different way. It also propelled me into a nomadic life in Europe, searching for a home, only to end up in a place called Piemonte, in the middle of nowhere, in the northwest corner of Italy nestled up against the Alps. It took me practically twenty years to find another home, but I did. My mother, Muv, whom I loved more than anyone, always had faith I would find my way even if I wouldn't go in a straight line. I could be a dilettante, but I would never have set off on my adventure were it not for my mother's secret; without it I couldn't have found my own.

The timing of Muv's confession, like her manners, was perfect. I was newly married to a man named Francis and looking forward to the rest of my life; I felt secure and well-loved. We were living in Seattle where Francis was working at Microsoft and I had just retired after devoting five years to building a technical recruiting company that provided resources to Microsoft and other companies requiring IT support. We were happy and felt deeply grateful.

Muv's revelation was like taking the Red Pill; it lowered the veils and changed my sense of reality. The year was 1999 and a new millennium was on its way, the Dow just hit an all-time high, the tech boom was winding down, and Google was about to digitize the world. But when Muv told me her secret, our secret, my sense of time faltered, as if too much had been lost. I felt like I had been released from her womb all over again.

We lived on the lake at the time and water can feel so emotional—we were completely surrounded by it. Our dock was composed of 20 houseboats, similar in size and shape, square and slightly bigger than most of the 400 homes floating on top of various bays and waterways surrounding the port city of Seattle. The lower story of our houseboat consisted of an office with a bed for guests and across the marbled corridor through another door was our master bedroom where I lay in bed.

I didn't want to wake up and kept my eyes closed, my body still. I felt a small wave, followed by another which was highly unusual because our home sat close to the land on a very heavy, flat slab of concrete. I must have been drifting in and out of sleep trying to re-capture dreams of someone carrying a message. Then another wave, heavier than the first, it rocked my body, forcing me to open my eyes. I found two small dogs sharing our bed, two Papillons; a breed named after their butterfly shaped ears. They were chosen specifically to fit into our new nautical lifestyle. Colette was securely perched on her little pillow right above my own in a concise, tight circle, ready to spring gracefully into action at a moment's notice. Colette's eye lashes didn't even flutter. Her brother, Godot, lay his head on Francis' pillow, facing away from me as if on guard. Godot was stocky. He assumed he was far larger than his size which was precisely twice that of Colette; together they weighed less than ten pounds and took up little space on our California-size Tempurpedic bed.

I glanced half-heartedly towards the window spreading the length of the wall, noting it was so early the sun had barely begun to streak the walls through the blinds. I thought about calling Francis, wondering whether he was still in London or en route to Tokyo. I imagined the view beyond the blinds. I had never felt the water before, not like that, perhaps a neighbor was out playing on his jet ski before going to work. Or maybe a group of canoe enthusiasts had paddled their way down our fluid alley. We had a small waterway in between the row of houseboats in front of us, four floating homes that boasted a better view. On the rare occasion I caught someone peering inside our windows, I'd flip the blinds open and watch them pretend to look elsewhere.

I left the bed to investigate, peaked cautiously through the blinds, and found the water unoccupied and stagnant beneath the porch. The lake looked calm and as I tried to push away the peculiar ideas swirling through my mind the sound of a phone broke through the silence.

I fell across the bed, picked up the receiver and heard my mother's optimistic greeting, "Good Morning!"

"This is an early call, what time is it?"

Muv said, "Oh darling, I'm so sorry, I just couldn't fall back asleep, so I thought I'd call, you don't mind do you?"

I rolled over onto my back and crossed my legs in midair and got settled. Talking with Muv was usually a comfortable affair and when it wasn't, the storm passed as quickly as it arrived. She apologized again, and suggested she come over for dinner. We signed off and then it dawned on me she never invited herself over for dinner. She was so private and never wanted to impose. I began to think that perhaps something was amiss but was interrupted by another call which made me feel like I was there to wait for instructions.

Without a greeting she said, "You know dear your father's not feeling too well, why not just the two of us. I can't wait to see your place, I just wanted to wait until it was done."

"How is—"

"And hey, listen" she cut me off, "you always go to such trouble, how about something simple, just salad, and some bread and maybe ice cream, how does that sound?"

I turned the receiver around and looked at the phone while she took my silence for acceptance, said good-bye and hung up. She sounded too eager and I wanted to call her back but the dogs jumped off the bed warning me it was time to take them out. Afterwards I took a shower and walked into my closet noting everything was where it should be as if this provided some relief from the tone in my mother's voice. Muv had her own sense of time and couldn't be pushed. I tried to shake the feeling of unease and suspected Muv would arrive to put everything at rest. She always did so I decided to head off to the Pike Place Market to shop for 'something simple'.

Muv was punctual and we air kissed at the door, laughing our way up the steps. At the first landing I said, "Now make sure you notice the photos on the wall," which was unnecessary because like most mothers she noticed everything. "Your old photographs are wonderful, I don't even remember this one."

"With five kids you don't leave them hanging around, you may never see them again."

"You know, I never thought about it until now, but you rarely talk about your past..."

She interrupted me, "You don't often ask and you're always moving so fast, I can't keep up."

I could feel there was something on her mind. "In case you haven't noticed I've spent the last six months fantasizing I'd inherited Grandfather's nautical skills but I think Francis has his doubts." As we walked around the first landing each step greeted us with a picture of my grandfather aboard one of his boats, always at the helm, dressed in casual, smart attire. Then the next showed five-year-old Muv and her twin, Phyllis, facing their older sister, Jane. Images from an ancient summer, their heads small and vague at the back of their 60 foot teak yacht. All three girls had summer hair, short and sun kissed. Three sisters with practically nothing in common even if two of them were fraternal twins.

"Now I understand why you didn't want me to invite Phyllis to the wedding," I said. "You know the first thing she said to me was, 'I haven't had a drink in two weeks. I lost 10 pounds for your wedding.' As if I was to blame."

"I know, I know. Each time I gave birth she became pregnant straight away."

"Remember the last time we visited Phyllis in Sacramento?" I asked. "She was drinking gin and tonics and wanted us to keep up and you didn't want to me to encourage her, and suddenly she starts singing, like she's performing in front of us. It was like we were in that movie, "What ever happened to baby Jane."

Muv wasn't going to be drawn into a conversation about

her twin and focused on the photos in a familiar way, "Oh I like the slim black wooden frames, they don't compete and the enlarged pictures turned out surprisingly well."

"I only remember meeting Grandfather Walter once."

"No, you were too young."

"He didn't like Dad much, did he. I asked him about Grandfather once and he said, 'I come from a long line of social climbers' like it explained everything."

"Yes, a smile and a handshake is your father's philosophy," she said absentmindedly. "Father was so fastidious you know, we wouldn't dare touch any of that brightwork, but oh, those summers spent in Sausalito were just wonderful."

Francis and I had recently flown down to buy a sailboat in San Francisco and I spent time with my mother's cousin Diana, who happened to have a passion for genealogy. She gave me a print out of her research but it only served to raise interest in my grandfather, rather than answer any questions. It felt like Muv's father was too carefully buried in her past.

I tried to tease her, "For someone who isn't fond of boats it sounds like you liked them once upon a time, and Diana was full of information."

Muv's reply seemed focused on something else. "Oh you mean about my father's previous life. I think I told you Grandmother Gertie was his secretary before they married."

"Well, Diana said grandfather had a relationship with a top socialite in San Fran and he might have had a family before yours, I mean, you're close with her, you know Diana isn't a fantasist, wasn't she the first female Superior Court Judge in San Francisco?"

"Alameda, dear, and she probably knows more about the family line the anyone. She's extraordinarily social and engaged, I'm happy you were able to spend time with her, she's always traveling, enjoying her opera everywhere, what a life."

"Diana remembers your father fondly, and so well, but it's like your previous life had a theme you don't seem to miss—weekly high teas at the St. Francis Hotel and luncheons at the Yacht Club. Did I tell you, I took our cousins to the club because we have reciprocity privileges at the Seattle Yacht Club, the difference felt almost exotic."

Muv was now interested, "Who did you take?"

I told her and said, "I don't know, maybe it's because I'm starting out on my new life with Francis and I'm curious, like I'm searching for some invisible myth and Grandfather Walter rarely gets a mention." I was standing on the stair beneath her, "I mean, weren't you ever curious about his life before you came along?"

Muv looked at me and quickly looked down, navigating the final steps. "Well, I suppose we all have our secrets." When she arrived at the upper story she spread her arms wide taking in the open space before her. "Oh! It looks fantastic, those birch floors change everything don't they, it's so light now!" Her tone began low, complementing the tile work and then she smiled and led us to the fireplace with exclamations. Her voice was warm and her words slowed down as she put her purse down and looked at me in conspiratorial fashion. "Now doesn't that rug just make the room."

I smiled because the Persian rug had been in our family forever. "I'm so happy it's all done." I walked over to the kitchen area. "And just because I'm a product of the 70's doesn't mean I have to live in it." I took out a bottle of Pinot Grigio from the small wine refrigerator and poured two glasses. I wanted her opinion, so I left her alone and turned my back to wash the lettuce in the sink. She remained silent so I assumed she was admiring the space; she could put a positive spin on anything.

"Well, I bought something simple for dinner. That was a strange request coming from you. Remember the duck pate you made as if it was the most natural item to sit next to the jello molds and store bought cookies at Brenda's 12 birthday party..." I glanced over my shoulder and caught her staring at me. I was confused at first then looked at her empty wine glass. I laughed because she must have thrown it back like a sailor, "You want another?"

At 65 she preferred tea over wine and smiled, "Oh why not," and I went back to the sink and laid the lettuce on top of a green linen napkin and started cutting the tomatoes.

Then, without warning, she blurted it out: "I had an affair." For a moment, I didn't recognize her voice. I turned my head, but the rest of my body wouldn't move. It felt like another wave swept underneath my feet. I tried to focus on a thought but they kept disappearing, the answer was dangling in front of me, but I couldn't grab it. I thought of my father who was surely entering dementia, and my brother Blaine whose brain tumor had returned. This must have been Muv's solution for our family slowly falling apart. She had an affair and the idea felt deeply romantic.

"Mother, you? I can't believe it, when?"

All I could see was a vertical line with a head tilted to one side. Then my mother's eyes opened wide with a child-like expression, "How old are you darling?"

∾

*...becoming the boxer's daughter*

∾

I STARTED to laugh but the shock cut me off. My hands clutched the edge of the sink. When I tried to catch her eyes she looked away, unwilling to watch the effect unfold on my face. For the first time I was at a loss for words and she was tripping over so many of them.

"Oh dear, why did I say that, I didn't mean it, honestly, it's everything, your brother moving back from Europe after such a short time when he seemed so happy there, at least with his job. Blaine's genius at retail, imagine getting a consulting job like that, he loved traveling and then his brain tumor came back, and here we thought they removed everything with the first surgery. Then Sally, I have to say, your neighbors must have heard her, I'm sorry, she just showed up, your sister was screaming at the top of her lungs in your house. Then your father, he just sits in his chair reading his book, and when I look up from my easel, I realize he hasn't turned a page in over an hour..." she trailed off, exhausted.

Her question threw me off and her words rattled my brain. "Why was Sally here? For heaven's sake it's taken me 33 years to cut her out of my life, she lies constantly. I let her in here once when we first moved in and that was enough."

Muv's response was spoken in slow motion, "She just showed up while I was housesitting, when you were in Europe, last month, she was demanding pictures of Blaine as if we were hiding them. It was very bizarre, I'm sorry I let her in but I had no choice."

This caused more confusion and I started speaking faster, "Why was she demanding pictures of Blaine? Are they planning a memorial?" I pressed my fingers against my forehead. My eyes needed a reprieve as I looked at the water, "Sally and I don't have any mutual friends, or interests, we don't look like sisters, our memories don't even overlap..."

my voice trailed off and the family faded away. Then it registered as my speech slowed down. "Maybe it wouldn't feel like this if everything around us wasn't unraveling...still, you, of all people had an affair, and a love child, and it's me? I never saw this one coming, I mean, mother, you are the essence of protocol, you're the only one in the room, certainly in this family, who always knows precisely the right thing to say and do."

I took my wine glass and walked around Muv. I caught her eyes blinking as if slightly taken back by her own announcement. She took one step backward as if waiting for me to give her a cue. This new territory was uncertain. I put my glass down on the bar and slid the stool next to me underneath, assuming she might appreciate a little distance. We looked at one another. The sun had moved behind the first row of houseboats giving the upper story a sympathetic ambiance and surrounding us in the color mauve.

Her voice was barely above a whisper, "I didn't mean it, it's not true, I don't know why I said it."

I ignored her attempts at erasing the truth but this sensation of being released from my mother's womb made me nervous. I said, "I've been waiting for you to talk about the past, because you rarely do. Is it because of me?"

Now she looked confused. "No, no darling, this has nothing to do with it, and it happened so long ago."

I couldn't resist. "Well, it sure feels recent to me," but my voice trailed off. Her secret had been successfully sent and carefully caught. The truth was written all over her face.

"Who is it?" She followed my lead and got settled at the end of the bar stretching her neck away from her long, disciplined figure. There's no denying we are mother and daughter, even though we're full of differences. Her limbs are long and defined by straight, flat plains whereas my body is full of curves, yet both are obedient, each have instructed us to move cautiously. Muv's about to announce his name when her left hand lifts up from the counter as if suddenly in need of a manicure. I'm strangely patient and even amused by her gesture. I want to laugh because this must be a joke yet I can sense my patience is a remedy for fear. I'm not even sure I want to know the answer.

She lowered her hand as her eyebrows lifted, "It's Victor, you remember who Victor is, don't you?"

I was suspicious. "Is this another question?"

Muv lowered her gaze, "No, it's your turn for questions. You must have many."

"You mean Victor as in the same Victor who happens to be Blaine's godfather?"

"Yes, they are one and the same."

I sat back and out came a heavy sigh, "Oh my God, that's interesting, isn't it. I'm going to have to let that one sink in."

"I just thought you should know, you deserve to know, this is so hard, I'm so sorry."

But I felt relieved, "Of course it would be Victor. It's almost as if we're connected again, we used to be so close until he got married. Then everything changed, didn't it?"

"It has been a challenge, yes."

I said, "His wife isn't just angry, she seethes. I felt she was creating stress long before Blaine was diagnosed with his brain tumor. And then the minute he found Jesus I had lost a brother."

I might as well have been talking to myself. Muv wasn't going to comment on my brother's marriage because there was nothing to be done. The more angry his wife and Sally acted, the more my mother resembled a tempest-proof pavilion. Parents aren't supposed to have favorites but mine did and there would always be a strong connection with

Blaine. Yet today she's focused on me with concern etched all over her face.

It's hard to concentrate but I force my attention back to what she's trying to tell me. "Well, ok, I'm glad it's Victor. He's been in our lives forever if only in the shadows. I'm grateful, Mother, really, it might even feel like a gift if it didn't seem like a grenade just went off inside my head."

"Darling, this is all too much for you, you're in shock."

"Well, our family has been falling apart for a long time. I almost feel vindicated about distancing myself from the drama. Maybe this shouldn't come as such a surprise, but it is, I mean I knew I was different, I just didn't ever think..." I noticed my glass was empty, "I need some more wine." I got up and decided to serve the bread with some butter and cheese. "You certainly took your time telling me. You're always so methodical."

Muv looked at me evenly for a long minute, "I did think of telling you before, then wondered if you might be a little prejudiced, or perhaps..."

"I just wasn't ready, I guess. The only thing I know about Victor is that we all like him. And he's a little older, isn't he?"

"You know Victor's Mexican and Basque, he has such a rich history, and he recently went back to Spain and spent time in the Basque country. I think it was quite moving for him." Muv continued to share details about Victor's experience with prejudice, incidents he shared with her, its effect on him and how much it impacted her. I listened but the information sounded superficial. I couldn't tell what had changed. Each time I asked a question she provided an answer and then a long silence followed. We nibbled on the baguette and ate all the ice cream. The salad went limp on the linen next to the sink.

I looked around me and my home felt too new, as if I

was trespassing in a house owned by someone else. The idea of Victor was too large and couldn't be contained in this space. I took my shoes off and said, "Let's move to the couch, it's so big it must have been meant for this night alone." What I really wanted was to be near that rug because it was the only thing in the room that felt familiar. Muv followed and I grabbed a pillow and laid down. She sat at the other end and motioned to put my feet on her lap. Every once in a while she'd rub the top of my foot, trying to be maternal.

I looked across at her, "Did you continue the affair after I was born?"

She quickly replied, "Oh yes, for about a year, we were in love."

I felt my body relax because I believed her, "Didn't he win some major boxing championship?"

Her face softened and became animated. "Yes! You know he was a Golden Gloves Champion for the Navy, this was considered the height of cool back then," she said this with the quickest wink and a smile, then added, "He also had a Ph.D. in philosophy from Stanford. You take after him in this way, so curious and smart."

I ignored her desire to pump me up. "He's friends with Charles Schultz isn't he? Don't they play hockey together in Santa Rosa?"

"They've been playing together for decades, they still play every week, I think they're very close."

For the first time in my life I could relate to Charlie Brown. The more details she provided the less real it felt. There was a layer between us I couldn't penetrate. Night arrived as the windows turned to black and intimacy returned. For the first time since she blurted out the truth I could relate to her again and said, "That's unbelievable, we both got pregnant with hockey players, I never thought we'd ever have that in common."

Muv sat wrapped in silence. We hadn't talked about my pregnancy in years. It happened over 15 years ago during my first year away at college. She had little problem with the birth but never liked the biological father. I had stayed in denial about being pregnant for so long that I ended up giving birth to a premature child. The story had been recycled so many times in my head and with friends it lay dormant, until now. Muv had warned me about this boyfriend and it was the only time we ever clashed; I should have listened because he was the wrong guy at the wrong time, but there was nothing either one of us could do about my hormones. She didn't even bother mentioning his name even though she was highly sympathetic about that time in my life. It was like an aberration.

Muv cautiously asked, "Aren't you ever curious about her?"

For the first time I smiled. "Didn't I ask you that same question earlier?" I welcomed the chance to change the subject. "By law I don't think I can be, at least, I've never explored the idea. I gave birth and I gave her up for adoption. I can't imagine wanting to disrupt her life again, I mean, I interrupted the natural cycle, and why do it all over again. If she's curious, she'll find me."

After a long pause I said, "I can't even relate to that person I used to be but maybe I can with my own daughter. Not only do I have a biological daughter, but a father as well, they're like my biological bookends." I said very slowly, "If I had not been so young and so stupid and stayed in denial the entire time I would have had an abortion."

Muv knew what I wanted to ask and shut her eyes and shook her head. She never would have contemplated having

an abortion nor would she have gotten pregnant with a guy
like Steve; I had nothing in common with the father except
for the deep initial attraction. Muv's decisions were made
with heavy consideration, whereas I was always impetuous.
Still, our affairs overlapped in my mind, and I began to feel
protective of her, perhaps in the same way she had been
protective of me all my life. We stared at one another as if
she knew what I was about to ask.

"Does Dad know?"

She answered immediately. "Oh no, he doesn't, it would
kill him if he knew. He adores you, you know that."

I was genuinely surprised. "He really doesn't know?"

Her answer was cryptic, "We've never talked about it."

I didn't have the energy to argue. If it was hard to believe
he wasn't aware of the truth it was easy to conclude they
never discussed it. I wasn't even sure what to believe because
it was too much to take in. I kept trying to remember what
Victor looked like but couldn't find his face.

I said, "You have a picture of his family on your wall,
don't you? Only you could pull that one off. Now I understand, and I'll pay attention next time I'm at your
apartment."

Muv was going to say something but I said, "It's almost
midnight and I'm exhausted." I wanted to be alone, or
thought being alone might help clear my mind and said to
her, "I'm going to be fine, really, I'm just glad you told me, I
don't have to go to work tomorrow, or next week, I have time.
Come on, let's get up. Dad will wonder what's happened to
you."

After she walked out onto the porch, I folded my arms
and leaned against the door jam. She said, "You know how
much I love you. Call me anytime, day or night."

I smiled. "Tsk, tsk, tsk." I wanted to tease her and make

light of the situation because she had always made me feel so comfortable; until tonight. "Oh, I almost forgot. Tomorrow's the big day. My neighbors have asked me to be supportive and go to the court hearing downtown. Can you believe that? They are so litigious. I keep asking them about the details of the lawsuit but the Board tells me they have everything under control."

Muv's expression finally changed and became deadly serious, "You better watch out, these Home Associations can create a lot of problems and they're always looking for a scapegoat, you don't want to set yourself up."

"I think I already have. Do you know when we moved onto the dock our monthly dues were 200 dollars? Six months later, we're paying 1,000 dollars a month because of legal fees. Isn't that amazing?"

Muv looked over at a neighbor's floating home then back at me, insinuating our conversation could carry across the water. I got her point.

Muv found her keys and threw me another surprise, albeit this one was much smaller, "I'm going to call Victor tomorrow and let him know I've told you."

I let out a small laugh knowing this was simply protocol for her.

She emphasized her parting comment, "Call me, day or night..."

I nodded and closed the door knowing beneath all her worry she was curious about the next move I'd make. She had kept the secret locked in a room for decades and now I had permission to open the windows and breathe freely and yes, I wanted to invite guests. I was feeling simultaneously terrified and rejuvenated by my new conundrum. It was time to try it on someone else.

I had warned Muv, "I need to tell Francis."

She gave me a weak response, "Oh please don't," she might as well have been talking to the air. "Whatever will he think of me?"

We knew it didn't matter as I took the stairs two at a time and flew by the photos with their ancient memories and rushed towards my future. I glanced at the kitchen and thought about pouring myself another glass of wine but I felt the emotional pull to call Francis, as if it could offer some form of release. My office was a small, triangular room isolated from the rest of the upper story. I sat down and looked at the keyboard as if it contained some kind of code. I tried in vain to break the cycle in my head. I started to dial the overseas number but was distracted by my reflection. A tiny lamp offered just enough illumination to inspect the contours of my face. At first it looked familiar until my image appeared as complicated as a Cubist portrait and I had to look away.

I dialed and Francis answered and after sharing the news I said, "I always suspected a Bohemian lay just beneath the surface, but not this."

He was intrigued by another angle. "You're part Basque, that's very cool are you familiar with the myth of Atlantis?"

"No, but to think I felt sorry for you because your mother is Italian, your father is German and you've lived in so many places—"

Francis interrupted me and said with pride, "I know exactly what I am, I'm Italian."

I laughed and appreciated his confidence. Francis was just starting his day and had to end our conversation. In bed, incapable of sleep, I kept wondering what had changed; what if I had known sooner? Would my choices have been any different? Would I have ended up here, married and living on a houseboat? Did I have a new identity? There had to be some way to eliminate the confusion. The only solution that came to mind was finding a way to revisit my past. I couldn't reconcile my previous life with the present so I needed to find a way to make them friends again. If I had to spend part of my day at the courthouse downtown the idea of a detour made sense. I could re-acquaint myself with the past and visit that girl I'd left behind. I recalled reading Joan Didion's essay about how important it was to remain on speaking terms with our previous selves. I could practically hear that little girl saying, "Take me with you, trust me, you'll need me." And a lunch with Norman, yes, that would help. He was my wise friend, the kind of friend who told me what I needed to hear instead of what I wanted to hear. Lunch with Norman was exactly what I needed.

## 2

## LOVE LETTER TO SEATTLE

❧

For the first time our bedroom investments offered no return value. Sleep never arrived and my Pilates machine couldn't straighten out my crooked back or sooth my scoliosis. My head was spinning and my body felt too tight. All bets were on Norman to straighten me out. When he answered the phone I said, "Can we meet for lunch?" Then I remembered the court case and said, "Actually, can we meet for dinner, it really is an emergency."

Norman responded calmly, "I'll make the reservation for 7:30."

I was grateful for good friends and set out for the day. As I stepped out the door onto our front porch I found Jerry standing inches away from my face. Jerry was President of the Home Association Board and took enormous pride in his position. His body was ram rod straight and his chin jutted out like he was confronting me when he was just asking for a favor.

"Good morning Bailey, great timing! I was about to

knock and make sure you were going to show up at the court hearing today."

Without a smile or greeting I shut the door behind me, "Well, I guess I'll finally get some answers on what this law suit is all about. After today, we're done, right? Whether or not we win?"

He moved back off the porch and onto the steps, "We'll see, and I'm sure we'll win, we have a strong case." With a small wave and a tight smile, "Have a great day!"

Unsure about my confrontational mode, I noticed a spring in my step as I waltzed into the garage. *Litigation has replaced sex for these assholes*, I thought to myself.

My neighbors fell into the future as I drove away in our savvy black Mercedes, though it might as well have been my old Honda with the broken back window. My body shifted into autopilot as my hand loosened on the wheel, my brain relaxed into a nostalgic mindset as I drove toward downtown Seattle, a space packed with memories.

I was going to find the keys to unlock my new mystery. Intuition suggested I treat the city like a first love and visit previous addresses and haunts, thereby re-visiting myself. What surprised me was the number of apartments; whenever finances allowed I'd pack up my things only to move six or seven blocks away. I navigated Seattle's cliques like a gypsy—if I wasn't meeting new people it didn't feel like I was moving forward. Seattle was full of cliques because people kept to their own intimate circles even if they overlapped for me. Everyone seemed to let me in, perhaps because they thought I wouldn't overstay my welcome.

I was always restless and too curious, always in search of a home. The various buildings and rooms melded into one as the city shifted into a specific shape. Seattle materialized as an intimate friend, intensely familiar, uniquely unforgettable, and informative in ways I'd never imagined. I wanted to relish every aspect of her contained space. Today she looked fantastic. When Seattle decides to show off, there's no need for pretense, draped in a casual summer ensemble. Couture is out of the question, and when the clouds part and the sun bursts through, the sky can't help but reflect all that water below. It's quietly magnificent and utterly welcoming. The city no longer feels discreet, but sparkles.

For a small stretch of time, she's all mine. It's a city eminently livable. Water was everywhere which should have created heavier emotional climes but Mount Rainier and the Cascades balanced her out; making her practically impossible to pin down. Seattle isn't a glamorous city. There's nothing particularly overt, and no wish to intimidate. She appears cozy and kind, or what could be construed as 'professionally nice'. Visitors might imply it's a veneer although I think it's based on social timidity. Some cities are defined by their politics but not Seattle, and old families never tried to impose; she's too mercurial. There's no hurry. It was never her intent to settle for little sister status to the city of San Francisco.

When our family moved from Napa Valley in the 60's I never heard Muv compare the two because she didn't think it was a competition. She thought Seattle would eventually come into its own. I always thought of Seattle and Silicon Valley as fraternal twins. For several decades Lockheed Martin and Boeing each benefitted from major investments from the Defense department. By the time the 90's skidded in, Seattle was so productive she was creating at least 35 percent of America's exports with Boeing being one amongst many of America's most influential brands.

Muv's forecast was right on. The Emerald City was no longer the bridesmaid. Just look at her dowry: Microsoft,

Amazon, Starbucks, Nordstrom, Adobe, and McCaw, not to mention the biotech firms. Considered an indoor city, people still read here more than in any other in the country and Seattle produced as many engineers as the numbers flocking from outside the state to Bellevue, Issaquah, Sammamish and other counties on the east side.

There was no shortage of entertainment in Seattle, with a surprisingly large amount of major and fringe theaters, second only to New York in the number of equity actors. Muv had tickets to three of the major theater houses yet the ballet was our Mecca and we never missed a performance. Everyone seemed intent on keeping the fringe theater circuit alive at this time, and I did my part to contribute to fundraising. Seattle was a patient city, suggesting the locals wait for musical trends to run their cycle. In the 40's and 50's the jazz craze hit Seattle and clubs lined up downtown and still fill Pioneer Square with a steady audience. In the 90's the grunge enthusiasts flocked downtown before settling permanently on Capitol Hill when Seattle's temperature returned to normal, which it always did.

Seattle survived the multiple financial boom and bust cycles in the same way musical swings came and went. She didn't need to be cool or kick up a fuss. Angst didn't fit with her temperament. Seattle's strongest trait and most natural tendency was to slide back into her steady self which was seriously industrious and socially reticent.

When local newscasters were given a chance at national exposure they did their time and took a test drive before returning to Seattle. Our sports teams were content to stay local after entering the national consciousness. When the Seattle Supersonics took the country by storm, they came back to play tennis on the public courts in Magnolia with kids like me. Of course I could be biased because our village was one of the prettiest in Seattle. It was called Magnolia and sat on a peninsula nuzzled right up against the city. With a long and winding bridge on one side and one of the steepest hills on the other, the place appeared secluded and idyllic. In fact JKF Jr. and his new wife Carolyn quietly checked out the real estate along Magnolia's bluff where my childhood summers were spent sunning on elevated decks high above the water.

Seattle kept steady and inspired people to settle down and start a family. "Well," I asked myself, "was I going to start a family?" When the subject of kids came up, which was rare, it flew out the window once Francis started talking about future travel destinations. He was a restless soul, always looking for the next adventure. Seattle was the place he lived the longest, until I started to disengage and started looking forward to those conversations about future travel. My personal goal of financial independence had been accomplished and the moss was no longer growing beneath my feet.

There was money to be made in a town full of entrepreneurs and while international visitors insisted she was too removed from the financial markets, I was convinced that this was specifically what made her special. Seattle was sought after even without having to perform spectacular feats to lure in new residents. Money didn't really seem to be the final prize. There was the odd Bentley, and a conspicuous bright red Ferrari, always the latest model, driven by my friend Michael Mogelgaard; but that was expected because he was an advertising maverick. Yet when you saw a Volvo, preferably green, you had to suspect success. Seattle was exploding and if timber had formed her beginnings, and natural resources kept her going, technology was fastening her within its eager grip. The city was no longer one of the country's best kept secrets. But for a precious minute, in 1999, she was still mine. I didn't even know I was preparing to say good-bye.

Seattle is also small. Within minutes I was at my last address, located at the corner of Olive and Boren, tucked right in between downtown and Capitol Hill. *I just moved and it feels like a lifetime ago*, I thought to myself.

My eyes combed the dirty beige building. I thought a casual observer might find it bland if it weren't for the gothic towers sprouting out from on top. My neighbors were gothic girls, transgender men, and a host of eclectic characters. The building carried the status of 'low income housing' but the top floor was excluded. If I hadn't taken advantage of the tech boom, I couldn't have lived in my little salon in the sky. Muv had given me the Persian rug and an embroidered parlor set she'd inherited from her parents. I played my piano with other musicians, but there was little time for happiness. It was all about work.

*...FROM DRAG QUEENS to engineers*

IN MY EARLY 20'S, a country club friend from my tennis days asked me to coordinate a few fashion shows at his nightclub on 1st avenue. He wanted to expand his clientele beyond the frat crowd. I said yes and started running around to all the downtown clothing stores asking if I could showcase their latest season. By day I frantically collected the clothes and went to various hair salons begging stylists to contribute their time for free at night. Everyone was game because no one else was doing it. Each week I came up with a new store and a novel idea. I started recruiting well-known dancers like Seattle's favorite, Wade Madsen, and he happily directed and starred in a couple of my runway shows.

I knew these events were popular when the drag queens started showing up. They'd find me standing next to the DJ booth praying the fog machine might work this time. They studied me, unsure I was the one responsible for these elaborate shows. Not sure what to make of them either, it dawned on me; they were the characters in a play I'd never written. I started visiting Larry Leffler, an old school drag artist who designed clothes and performed on public television. His performing days were over and his apartment was weirdly enchanting, pieces of old costumes carefully strewn about, some dolls, and other collectable items. He listened to my idea and encouraged me to interview some of the locals and create a show.

I'd been enjoying plays at our local theaters since I was twelve years old and dreamed of becoming a playwright. I loved staged drama and started to write a script highlighting the performers and their individual acts. There was Mandonna, Diana Ross, a young, gregarious guy called 'Boy Mike' who nailed Roseanne, and another performer who did an uncanny impression of Lucille Ball in her famous Vitameatavegamin skit. Toni James was instrumental in making this show a success. Toni had produced shows for the Seattle Men's Chorus and whenever I questioned my intentions he ways right by my side to lend confidence. I would say, "Do you think I know what I'm doing?" He simply replied, "Oh yes, I do." He was a professional. Everyone was exploiting the kitsch value but I thought their talent was immense and should be both celebrated and elevated. Their make-up created magic and their impressions were transfixing. A couple of them, in particular, Toni

James, would move on to well-paying jobs in Vegas, but until then it was just a local show I created called "Talking TV."

It was low on production value but high on entertainment. The movie, "Priscilla, Queen of the Desert," hadn't been released and Ru Paul was far from mainstream. I was asked to open for Ru Paul when he was in town but it turned me off show biz. I wasn't prepared and hadn't secured the necessary contracts and managed to get everyone paid but me. I also produced major events for Seattle's beloved Pike Place Market and other major retailers. My brother Blaine hired me to produce runway shows for Helly Hanson, to entertain and inspire clothing reps when they came to town. I hired rappers and dancers before rappers were rapping about fabric. The work was great but I never could figure out a way to make enough money to pay beyond the rent. Show biz just was not my style and it was time to close down this chapter in my life. I visited a few performers in the hospital who would die of complications from the AIDS virus. It was never meant to be a long-term proposition, and when you're a dilettante, nothing really ever is.

That's when I had the idea to move on to engineers. I was thrown out of my comfort zone when I started working for a guy named Bob. Our office was on Mercer Island which meant I had to drive across a floating bridge each morning. The island sat right between downtown and Bellevue, the largest city on the East side. It felt like a new frontier.

Practically every waking moment was spent building a consulting company. Bob was a classic IBM character from Philadelphia's mainline until Boeing offered him a job and transferred his family to Seattle. He was outsourcing nurses and selling coffee with little success. I was a glorified secretary who became bored and suggested he recruit technical engineers. He was skeptical until I started knocking on Microsoft's door before card keys came into play. I kept knocking. Eventually Microsoft let me in and I placed a few engineers. Each manager had his or her own fiefdom and each was trying to build it faster than the guy in the next office. Bob was still skeptical but he enjoyed putting ads in the paper and building a small database.

There was never really a plan but it didn't seem necessary because the tech industry was exploding. I gave our company a new name and spent all my time focusing on Microsoft because the construction was insane. Everyday I knocked on the door of a new building and marketed my best engineers. My eagerness matched their competitive behavior and they couldn't hire contractors fast enough to fill up all those buildings. I realized it was time to become acquainted with their internal Human Resource department. I navigated that department in the same way I navigated Seattle's cliques. We were small but they allowed us to become a preferred vendor early in the game. If I had any charm, it was used on them.

In the beginning, it was just me, my dog Ginger, and Bob. Five years later we had over 200 developers working at Microsoft along with various software companies and a few banks. I procured the clients, recruited, and most importantly, managed to retain the engineers. Or what we called 'techies' back then. If they wrote the code, supported the code, or analyzed it, I was placing them at Microsoft. Bob stayed in the office and expanded our database. He was technical whereas I knew the art of attaching a technical resume to the needs of the client. Bob's humor was an acquired taste, to be kind, and he could rub people the wrong way, but it was the perfect setting for me.

I could get anyone to talk about anything and most people liked to talk about themselves which was fine by me. Time was either spent in the field uncovering places where techies congregated, or at my salon in the sky dialing numbers and accumulating resources at night. Eventually I had a team of recruiters which allowed more time to procure new clients and make sure our engineers were happy. Most often they were not; rates and future possibilities were constantly discussed. There was always an engineer to take to lunch and there was always a new client to take to dinner.

I only took one day off and that was because I was forced to have my gallbladder removed. The following day I was at work, hunched over, my employees thought I was crazy. They had no idea what it took to grow a company. Unfortunately, little effort was devoted to making sure I was made partner. Bob thought my yearly bonus should suffice. For a while it did until it became apparent he never had any intention of making me partner. So I left.

We both felt betrayed but I was relieved. I was exhausted. It proved impossible to replace me and six months later he sold the company, took his winnings and moved back east. I didn't mind. Sitting there in my car I realized in some tiny way I was responsible for changing the composition of the city. I recruited hundreds of people from other cities and other countries. For this small stretch of time I felt uncertain about starting another company. I had several consultants who would follow me anywhere but could I do it again? I wasn't even sure who I was.

More importantly; did I have any fun? That was a loaded question. Outside the rare dinner party or baby shower, there were few memorable events in my salon in the sky. But the few were memorable. The time I threw a holiday business soiree I was surprised how many 'techies' showed up. It was probably the first and only time they came to Seattle so we both threw caution to the wind. I hired a local chanteuse named Julie Cascioppo who serenaded them in her version of Santa Claus in drag. If you ever managed to catch her act downtown, in between songs she wove in cryptic details about her life, but you suspected the sad bits were fact and the happy parts were fiction so you were never quite sure when to laugh. The audience simply had to ride the emotional roller coaster until the bittersweet end and the Julie Cascioppo experience was one they rarely forgot.

*At least my curiosity had a rhythm*, I thought to myself as if curiosity was a key clue. And I realized Julie Cascioppo and the drag queens were my stepping stone to recruiting engineers. It seemed natural to transition from drag queens to technical engineers because they both required strong advocates. They had similar personalities; they all acted like divas and each was devoted and completely convinced their area of expertise was superior. They both sat on the peripheral of society. The myth that mainstream ruled the world and the rest of our culture consisted of sub groups still existed. To my eyes, the world of engineers remained as invisible as the drag queens. Still, it had become a mad race to fill the technical positions. But eventually my clients stopped throwing money with reckless abandon at IT projects, it was increasingly difficult to place top level project managers; and it also became apparent the party was winding down in 1999. I was too.

I thought about how natural it felt to move from my apartment on 3rd Avenue to another on 4th, during the years I spent producing fashion shows and drag shows. Then I thought about how natural it felt to recruit engineers and move into that apartment on the corner of Olive and

Boren for three highly intense years. Perhaps Muv kept the truth from me because I was too busy. There wasn't much time to review whether or not I was happy. Then I remembered one Sunday morning when Seattle's mild weather managed to create high drama. The fog rolled in so thick it created a solid border at the floor below spreading itself evenly across the city and across Puget Sound. The effect was ethereal. Perfectly white air hung temporarily along the edge of each deck surrounding my little salon in the sky, offering the illusion of being in heaven. I stared out the window thinking, *This must be what it feels like to arrive*, and tried to trap the moment before it vanished.

# 3

# CLUES AND PATHOLOGIES

~

One memory was more reliable than the others
because they made a movie out of it called "The
Battle in Seattle." The 'Battle' was a series of
protests surrounding the WTO Ministerial Conference in
1999, when members of the World Trade Organization
convened at the Washington State Convention and Trade
Center, and created mayhem not too far from my apartment
building. It was a well-documented event that garnered
international attention. I just happened to have a front row
seat and spent one evening fleeing from one terrace to the
next, craning my neck over the ledges, watching the WTO
fiasco play out seventeen floors below.

In one catastrophic day Seattle changed dramatically.
Protesters arrived from across the globe to make a major
political statement intent on shutting down the city. Their
task wasn't difficult because Seattle always shared an
awkward relationship with protesters. It was not well
equipped for manufactured drama. I knew the man of the

hour; Chief of Police, Norm Stamper. For five years I sat on the board for 'New Beginnings'; a shelter and program to help eliminate domestic violence. Living in Seattle invariably inspired one to engage and volunteer for a non-profit because this was expected in a philanthropic city. Norm Stamper had come to our organization, specifically and Seattle, in general with plenty of experience, not to mention emotional intelligence.

But this new style of protest managed to both overwhelm and showcase the ramifications of globalization. And this day felt deeply up close and personal. It was hard to differentiate between the organic protestors and groups who were secretly funded. The chaos was too swift. The police figured the only option was to shift action from downtown up towards Capitol Hill. For hours the drama unfolded below our building. The intimacy of my city was disappearing behind tear gas; Seattle took on a sinister tinge with this quaint trait dimming before my eyes. Clashes were happening and locals were invariably caught in the midst, even my father was hit by tear gas running an errand on 1st avenue earlier that morning. I think Seattle lost its innocence that day. This was a year of surprises.

A few months later, I woke up one morning and realized my black Jeep Wrangler had been stolen. A vehicle both ideal and vital in my late 20's; I felt safe and indestructible driving it. Before paychecks went electronic, I used to hand deliver them bi-monthly to the 'techies'. It was a nice touch and they looked forward to the sight of my black jeep skidding into the various parking lots. I had memorized the maze of newly manicured gardens and drove through dozens of buildings scattered across the east side. When a female engineer said, "Bailey, because of you, I bought my first house," it meant the world. And it was rare because the industry was increasingly competitive. My jeep was like a weapon and I wanted it back.

The police found it a few days later. A couple of meth-heads had taken it for a joy ride then left it abandoned without any damage. The meth-heads also happened to be living three stories below my own. I found this out when a couple of goth girls told me. I was asking around and the meth-heads were causing trouble for other residents as well. However, my first attempt at confronting the group of young men was stupid and reckless. One morning I stepped out of the elevator on my way to work and found the young thieves arriving from a long night out. We'd never been formally introduced but I knew it was them, distinguishable by their eyes, menacing, enlarged black pools, eerily lit up, glaring, feeling little need to respond to my accusation. "I know you stole my jeep." They let their heavily dilated eyes speak as they silently walked around me, closely, slowly, daring me, staring until the elevator doors closed.

That night I bought a taser and the following day I went to the police station. I found the cop who filed the original report. "No, I don't have any hard evidence, but I know who stole my jeep."

This wasn't a Seattle cop, he was from New York, an Italian-American full of do's and dem's. He was open to my concerns and was charmed when I told him about a recent trip to Italy. I could be convincing when necessary and the following week the meth heads were gone. I knew the cop was responsible and took him to dinner which he appreciated. During our second bottle of Dolcetto, I asked him, "How did you do it?"

He shrugged his shoulders, "I just stopped by, saw all the paraphernalia laid out and we had a little chat."

Three years later, sitting in my Mercedes, my eyes went

from the salon in the sky that was no longer mine to the hands on my lap. I sat there and counted the number of friends taking Prozac and ran out of fingers. Seattle may be an internal city but it's as trendy as any and watching its effect let me in on a secret; that drug was anything but benign. I was comfortable with emotional highs and lows but for now the die had been cast. The pharmaceuticals had us in their grip or at the very least, they were on their way.

I also introduced Muv to Francis in that apartment. The moment I met him I knew he was the one; it was an epiphany. We were introduced in the corridor of one of Microsoft's buildings and I didn't want the conversation to end. When it did I walked away shaking my head in disbelief, "I can't believe he's the one." Francis was upside down original; he didn't look or sound like anyone floating in my orbit. A cerebral guy with the widest set of reference points I'd ever encountered, along with a few accents that would come in handy later on. If I needed a definition of any word, Francis was my encyclopedia. He didn't resemble the marketing guys from my past, he wasn't physically fit, and I highly doubt he ever once entertained the idea of visiting a gym.

I was nervous about introducing him to my mother knowing well she could size up anyone in a minute. I needed the scene to be festive and invited a few people over, and when they met I kept my distance. They appreciated this but I grew impatient and made an excuse to talk to Muv alone. She assured me, "Of course I get it darling. Completely. Now go take care of your guests." I did and Muv went back to chat with Francis.

～

IT WAS time to go to the courthouse. I took the elevator and found the room. It was sterile, small and white offset by the brown benches. I saw my neighbors shuffling in their coveted row anticipating the case. They pretended to note my arrival with approval but I decided to sit in the back row. I had a feeling this was not going to end well. For six hours we listened to petty details about stolen golf carts and personal insults. I found myself gripped by guilt, but couldn't figure out why. *I used the golf cart to transport the paint. Maybe I didn't return it the next day, did they think I stole it?*

I was completely confused and the judge was just mad. It was obvious to her the lawsuit was more of a personal spat between the Home Association and the developer who had built our parking garage across from the floating homes. If there were issues, they weren't necessarily legal, but intensely personal. The judge made it known her time had been wasted and it came as no surprise that we lost the case. She also made me wonder how much more time could be lost with this litigious group of neighbors.

"Before I announce the verdict," the judge said wearily, "I really suggest you people get a life." I saw two of my neighbors arch their backs. I looked for a quick exit.

Jerry was stuffing his notes into his small black briefcase trying to suppress his anger. I wanted to avoid him but he was standing at the desk below the Judge's bench. On the way to the door I cautiously said, "Gosh, what a surprise, that's bad news."

He looked at me as if it was my fault for asking so many questions in the first place. He gave me the same tight smile he wore that morning, "Oh don't worry, we're going to appeal. We have a lawyer on the dock, you know Jim, don't you?"

Jerry was well aware our home sat directly opposite from Jim's houseboat. It was common knowledge Jim had recently suffered a nasty divorce after coming out of the closet. Jim's late night calls with his ex-wife carried strong emotions across the water. His speedboat had *"Yes, dear,"* spelled out in large letters below the propeller. I walked out of the courthouse and seriously contemplated what it would take to put our houseboat on the market. By the time I reached my car I knew we would move off the dock.

## 4

## THAT GIRL

~

W hen I reached the water and took a right onto 1st Avenue I thought about visiting Muv at the other end when suddenly my senses height- ened. My old carefree life came back in the same way a kitchen provides the promise of a favorite childhood dish. Even my skin felt younger. Driving up to that elegant apart- ment from my distant past I knew it was safe because my roommate moved out long ago. Our paths never crossed; her social circle was very small and she had enemies. The relief of being released from the confines of the courthouse made me laugh out loud. The nostalgia was so palpable I realized this must have been that girl I left behind. Maybe she was one who could make my past and present friends again. I glanced up at that glamorous two-story apartment and thought, *Once upon a time it was packed with the prettiest clothes I'd ever seen.*

I met this roommate while studying at Seattle University. After my pregnancy I transferred my credits to Seattle U., as we called it, and got back on track. I thrived and was happy being back in the city. I did well in my studies and became completely engaged with the campus and won the lead for the spring theatrical production of James McLure's "Laundry and Bourbon." One of my professors had suggested I act in a play before trying to write one.

I struggled through rehearsals until the director pulled me aside and said, "Where is that young woman who gave such a provocative reading?" I too wondered where she had gone. The director, Bill Dore, was a well known local actor and knew his craft. He was worried until another actor suggested we spend a few nights after rehearsal just talking on stage and getting me to relax. Somehow I pulled it off but it taught me I was better served behind the scenes.

Muv knew I benefitted from the small campus as well as a fantastic education provided by the Jesuits. We were Episcopalian which meant I was 'Catholic Light' and I loved the mandatory philosophy courses. This idle thought made me think of Victor and this phase inspired a semester abroad at the University of London. We lived in apartments located one block from Harrods and there was a dream-like quality to the experience. My internship included a stint at a fringe theater in the east end where I fell in love with a struggling actor named Liam. I wanted to stay in London but Muv said I had to pay for it so I became a bar wench at a pub called The King and Keys on Fleet Street. In the early 80's journalists and printers were still devoted to the famous street, and in particular to this pub.

The proprietor was named Andy and the only day I saw him sober was the day he hired me. Andy, 'the Guv' would stand on a ladder near the bar where I served gin and tonics in large goblets and yell insults to his patrons as they entered the front door. The edgy aspect of the pub was balanced by good natured writers and a sweet gentleman who wore a bowler hat. He wrote me villanelles with titles like, "The Californian girl with the light blue eyes." I got tired of saying I was from Seattle because no one knew where it was, or if they did they would slightly dismiss it by saying, "Oh, you mean the other Washington". The experience had its charms but 'the Guv' was hard to deal with on a daily basis, especially when the drink continued late into the night. Once I began traveling to Paris and the continent, the seed had been firmly planted; I had fallen in love with Europe. Seattle was still home, and I returned happily, but I was more impatient than ever.

I left Seattle U just ten credits shy of my degree. This didn't please Muv who was paying for the expensive privilege but I was too tempted by a job offer at a publishing company. Seattle is known for many things but publishing isn't one of them. The publisher created a successful series of cookbooks from cities across the country and I eagerly accepted the job and loved the work. I helped coordinate the editors and the typesetters and I even got Muv in on the game. The owner was too cheap to pay her but she provided the most elegant little etchings of vegetables and herbs at the end of each chapter; she almost forgave me for leaving University early. The owner began spending the evening chasing me around the desk. He never had any intention of catching me but there was something devious about his method, as if he enjoyed testing my naive confidence which I seemed to have in spades.

I left the publishing world in the same way I left London, and moved into that glamorous apartment on 1st Avenue. It was a gorgeous two story apartment, located a few blocks from Pike Place Market, called The Grand Pacific Building. I decided to shift gears and develop a personal style because I didn't have one. I needed a lesson in how to wear clothes. To learn about finesse through line and fabric. When I met Tatiana at Seattle U., she was older, busy finishing her post graduate degree in business and wanted to open a designer clothing store. She was a tenacious blonde and former model with a prickly personality. I moved into her apartment and became her friend and employee. The store's opening night was grand and the adventure had begun. I was attracted to strong personalities because I could maneuver around them by never challenging them. My new boss and close friend could be ice cold, but she warmed up to me because I was game and did not compete. I offered a malleable presence letting her dictate the terms assuming my lesson wouldn't take too long. I just wanted to learn how to wear pretty clothes. Tatiana's mother was a Czech designer with an impressive CV, including working for major designers in Europe. Now she lived on the east coast and sent dozens of creations each season to the store.

During the day we worked at the dress shop; at night we played along 1st avenue and around the market. The clientele was composed of successful attorneys and women in white collar jobs working downtown. Savvy and stylish women with enough disposable cash to afford their own collection of high end crafted business suits and dress wear. The history of fabric was fading away in our disposable society but I got a glimpse of how fine it could be. Once or twice we took the trunk shows to New York, but Seattle was our milieu and those were halcyon days. It was the most superficial time of my life.

Tatiana was a hard-core salesperson and applied the same energy to evening pursuits. I played companion for dinner and drinks but someone had to open the store. The only pressing choice arrived before coffee. Should I wear the black wool crepe dress or the taupe wool crepe suit with the A-line skirt that seemed to move on its own, and hang so beautifully, soft, the lining barely there. Pieces of the various collections were scattered throughout our closets, dozens of silk blouses with bright, elaborate patterns, Egyptian cotton button down shirts, suits cut to perfection. It was an introduction to style I could never afford on my own and left a lasting impression. High end ensembles as carefully constructed as any seen along my travels later on, including couture shows in Paris. The future felt far away and responsibility lurked everywhere but there; the only obligation was to pay the rent. She kept my salary low and paid for most of the rent; it was a special deal to keep me at a disadvantage and one I didn't really mind at the time.

A series of exuberant exclamation marks jumped up from nearly every page of my early 20's. A trivial slice of life, highly social, and long forgotten until it became an ideal distraction after the courthouse experience. I'd forgotten how much fun it was to live in the middle of the city and let the vibrations drive a youthful body. My tastes were anything but epicurean yet were steadily remedied by hanging out in Seattle's best bistros and finest restaurants. My city was still intimate, run by locals who replenished its essence with their own flavor.

I was fortunate to have a friend like Michael Mogelgaard when I was 21, one of Seattle's central characters, the advertising maverick, because he treated me like a protege. However, being a dilettante he never hired me, but he did take me to dozens of restaurants around town; I couldn't have explored and embraced the diversity of our city's dining establishments at that age if it weren't for him. Mogelgaard was a colorful personality with a classic yet eccentric fashion sense to match, a man about town who happened to own one of the most stylish homes in Seattle. It wasn't large, just perfect. It was the kind of home talked about because there was nothing else remotely like it; an oasis in Seattle, the antithesis of the McMansions popping up on the East side. He threw my 30th birthday party in his avant-garde dwelling, which was a swell fest, but it couldn't possibly compare to the grand extravaganza he threw each year during Seattle's summer bash called 'Seafair'. Seafair is a slice of summer when Seattle steps outside its introverted self, gets completely inebriated and anyone in possession of a boat suddenly finds they have a thousand friends.

Mogelgaard's home allowed his guests to be greeted by curved walls covered in milky white, without a socket to distract from the dreamy effect. Inside, several grand French doors were tucked in between pictures windows with massive amounts of glass, with so much window space this sort of design could no longer materialize under today's regulations. During his annual Seafair Party the guests were given their cue when the earth began to move, when they knew they must leave all the internal eye candy and venture outside to the large deck. Lake Washington feels not only close but within reach. The eyes follow the landscape, a long wall of snow capped mountains called 'The Cascades' loom above with Mount Rainier sitting majestically to their side. With drinks in hand, laughing and standing under- neath, the jets arrived so fast and flew so low we can make out the goggles worn by the Blue Angel pilots in the cockpit. The next door neighbor decorated the side of his house with an American flag so large the jets aim for it throughout the afternoon, skimming the deck and the guests, the noise deafening and so dramatic we forget about all the artistic treasures inside.

Then, a clue, a dinner party from that section of my past, when Mogelgaard's home glowed like a tasteful art installation. It comes back like a dream but it was real. We're sitting around a long, glass table in the dining room, enveloped by walls painstakingly hand painted in black arabesque design, perhaps the aim was Florentine but the effect is delightfully eccentric. The dinner crowd is sharp and engaging, we're eating and drinking and competing with conversation, until a couple of us splinter off to relax and play an innately American game. That game where we ask each other about our ancestors, pretending we're still German or French even though it doesn't matter because we're quintessentially American, surrounded by the same cultural reference points that uniformly shape us within her borders, giving us a binary quality. The game gives us texture and Mogelgaard's art director is seated to my right and he's curious about my background.

When he asked I hesitate, "I think I'm German and Irish," and then repeat it as if to confirm my ancestry but he's not buying it and replied in a canny fashion, "Really? I see something else entirely." And so he had, and, he lost interest and looked away as if I should have known better. These memories offered additional clues from my past, and Seattle was ideal for me at that time of my life. When my body was resilient, engaged in periodic gluttony but it wasn't as if I was heading into an inferno; it was just fun to be young. During this idle slice of my life Muv watched from afar, wearily, perhaps she thought of Tatiana as a bit of a predator. Eventually my savior came in the form of a handsome PR executive named Tom. Looking back it appears I dated several Toms because they must have been reliable with such a sensible name. I moved into this Tom's home only to realize I didn't need to be saved; I just needed a dramatic excuse to release myself from a controlling drama queen that I could no longer handle.

Those were the days when I felt an excuse was necessary but now that I was the boxer's daughter, I felt emboldened in a small way. Or maybe my strength was evident all along and I just needed a refresher course.

# A NIGHT AT THE BALLET

~

Back then I didn't want to relish Seattle; I wanted to devour her. In particular the city's most prized real estate, the Pike Place Market, probably the oldest continuously operated public farmer's market in the country. I drove by on my way to meet Norman and thought of all that time spent familiarizing myself with every inch of the market. It was a steep building composed of several levels and restaurants hidden along ledges overlooking Elliot Bay or tucked further back behind the famous flying fish stall. These flamboyant fish mongers drew the tourists downtown yet the entire place was like a treasure hunt. It was a complicated endeavor to find places like the sexy dark French restaurant, "Shea Chez." You had walk up and down steep stairs and explore in the dark before finding the seductive bistros hidden down below.

I was to meet Norman at The Queen City Grill, the place where my relationships began and improved over time. It's where I graduated from cigarettes and martinis in my 20's, to lunching with ladies and eating spinach salad with a glass of chardonnay. It's where I took clients for late night dinners and where I ate oysters and drank Veuve Clicquot on my first date with Francis.

It was also where I got to experience lunch with Norman Durkee on a regular basis. I was lucky. Norman was a local treasure. He was like a humble Houdini who knew the secret combination. He was well known for writing and performing musical scores for marquee names and local plays as well as the ballet. He wrote catchy jingles for national commercials and when international exhibits came to town Norman was called upon to compose the score. He worked as a studio musician for years, on rock and roll anthems like, "Taking Care of Business," famous for writing his part on the back of a pizza box and playing it perfectly the first time. Barry Manilow and Bette Midler begged him to go on tour but no, Seattle kept him industrious and perfectly content.

Occasionally an artist or ad guy would enter and see Norman at our regular table next to the front window. They'd bow deeply or get on their knees then look suspiciously my way, wondering why I got to spend so much time with Norman. He once said, "It's because you're cute and fun," but I was also punctual and paid the bill every other time. I knew theater and why he incorporated the style of Kurt Weill heavily into his musical scores whenever possible; I knew my Bertolt Brecht.

I was early and stood at the bar talking to the bartender when Norman walked in precisely at 7:30. You couldn't miss him—large and imposing with a full head of frizzy grey hair cascading half way down his back highlighted by a dark uniform worn everyday in each season. A black wool jacket and matching pants with a custom-made white shirt. One time he offered me the name of his tailor but I declined. His face was semi-occupied by eye glasses thick with black rims. Below a prominent nose a long grey beard went half way down his chest and he never wore a tie; utterly relaxed Norman forever appeared like the casual composer. He saw me immediately and offered the softest smile. I rose to meet him at our regular table situated in an alcove. Everything about Norman was larger than life including a pair of immense grey blue eyes that twinkled, anticipating a colorful dinner and specific details regarding my emergency.

The minute we sat down I dove into my story and ended with Muv's question, "How old are you darling?"

He studied my face with his usual calm and said, "I always thought you looked a little like Paloma Picasso."

I sat back and the waiter arrived. We always ordered the same thing; salad with Shiitake mushrooms. I ordered another glass of Chardonnay and Norman ordered his Pellegrini sparkling water with a slice of lemon. Why should our lunch be any different from dinner? Nothing had changed.

I was frustrated by his response and threw up my hands, "That's it?"

Like my mother, he couldn't be rattled and like most musical geniuses he was highly mathematical with a methodical mind. He put his napkin on his lap and looked at me and said, "Why do you think she decided to tell you now?"

"I think it's because my brother is going to die and the family is a mess. It's her way of putting something right. You've met her. She's so private and reserved and she doesn't like to make anyone feel uncomfortable. The problem is I just don't know what's changed even if everything feels like it has."

Norman's life was full of characters and bizarre stories. He often brought them to the table. He wasn't just talented; he had funny stories about friends and he also helped his friends when in need. "Do you feel any different?" he asked quietly.

"Yes and no, the secret felt like a death of some kind, but it also felt like a new beginning."

Norman said, "Sometimes I wondered if things were as you said about your family. And sometimes when we met for lunch I knew I was an escape from your work. You didn't love it because it didn't seem to love you back. And the money didn't really seem to make you happy but then money never does."

I quieted down, "I know, money doesn't. Francis was very supportive when I quit. And to be honest, I was naive about my family, or maybe everything changed when Blaine became sick, and then converted. I went out to see him at his office a year ago, I thought we could talk about a recent event that alarmed my mother. His wife would call her and I don't know how to explain these...incidents, anyway it was awful. When I walked in I saw that sense of pride come over his face and then 5 minutes later I knew it was a bad idea. The temperature in that room changed so fast. I got up, I told him I loved him and that was the last time I saw him. As if I knew it would be the last time."

Norman continued, "I'm very sorry to hear about your brother, I didn't know he was that sick. I remember when you told me about his conversion. It's not easy. I think I told you about my father. He was a missionary and brought jello and bras to the Congo. You need to be careful. These people have an agenda and they can be disingenuous."

If Norman was trying to put a light spin on our topic I knew he was serious and replied, "Well, he's going to die and I'm not getting an invitation to see him before he does. I think part of the reason she told me the truth was because of all the pressure. Maybe I should go see Blaine and leave a card, and a flower, or something, my mother's cousin Betty recommended I do this, perhaps it could help..."

Norman was a gentle giant and I usually loved his thunderous laugh but not this time. When he laughed his head fell back and traveled south until the table got in on the act. I thought he was being cruel but I knew he was trying to make a point.

"OK, OK, I get it. They have an agenda. Going out there isn't going to change anything. Blaine is so angry I think he blames our mother for not being able to save him, to find the right doctor. Everything is such a mess."

He had stopped laughing when I looked around self-consciously, and said quietly, "I told you, my father was a missionary and I'm trying to shake you loose, Bailey, you're wound very tight. Maybe you should give yourself a break." The trouble with Norman was he always told me what I needed to hear not necessarily what I wanted to know. He continued, "It must be difficult being you because the inside is so different from the outside. I always wondered whether you were as confident as you appeared."

I tried to laugh, "Yes, there's an internal debate going on, I don't know who to believe, me or myself. Do you think I'm heading for a breakdown?"

"Do you?"

I answered, "No, no. It's not like that, I'm grateful because it feels like it answered a lot of questions I had, but didn't feel the need to address."

Norman asked, "You and your mother have season tickets to the ballet, don't you?"

I responded, "Front row center, we never miss it."

"Well, you can see me on center stage and if you want I'll let you backstage at intermission."

"Oh! We would love that Norman."

"This is my one night away from rehearsal and I have to go soon," he said. "Don't be so hard on yourself, you always are, it will just take time and you'll be fine. Just remember, Bailey, everyone's doing the best they can."

Norman was the only person who could pull off a comment like that and make it believable. Unfortunately, my dinner with Norman didn't have the soothing effect I craved. Apparently it was his invitation backstage that was necessary, and when Muv and I attended a night at the ballet, it not only proved a treat, it provided me with a lesson.

Norman was spectacular on stage, stark in three shades; black, white, and grey, the effect highlighted by pink and white ballerinas dancing around his grand piano. At intermission we were allowed backstage. At first, I felt like I was trespassing amongst the goddesses, as if disturbing their artistic space. Some of the dancers were slumped against a wall with feet flat, their magical energy in reserve. Before long, the aura of what I'd seen on stage began to slip away— I couldn't wait to get back to our seats.

Muv, on the other hand, was experiencing something entirely different. I thought she was standing next to me until I found her lurking in the shadows, observing and savoring every minute. I was reminded of a drawing she did along the length of my dining room wall in the penthouse. I asked her to paint a large mural and we decided to re-create the famous ballet rehearsal painting by Edward Degas' called "Rehearsal at a scene."

She'd chosen soft pastels in periwinkle blue and soft ochre expecting the next renter would paint over her work.

It was a perfect rendition, with its unique sense of imme-diacy and heightened perspective. Though when you looked closer, the ballerinas were slightly longer and thinner, reflecting Muv's favorite models of the 50's like Suzy Parker and Dovima. It was as if her drawing let her re-visit her previous life as a fashion illustrator on Market Street in San Francisco, the year before she got married and began an entirely different life. She was noticed early on and invited to a prestigious art school but her mother wouldn't pay for it even though money was never an issue. Muv had always done the right thing but for one moment she rebelled, and she was perfectly happy with the result, which happened to be me.

Now I watched Muv surrounded by ballerinas happily ensconced in her own Degas moment. In that instant she became my muse even though she always made me feel like it was the other way around. When we finally returned to our seats, I was relieved. We were so close we could see the ballerina's faces and finer details, their feet jumping against the boards. Front row seats offered just enough distance to feel the magic and admire the discipline at the same time. At the end of the performance, per usual, my mother was quietly ecstatic as she clapped like a child, her fingers straight, a smile washing over her entire face. Her enthu-siasm was infectious, and she turned away from the artists every now and then, to me, shaking her head, offering a wink.

For six years we attended the ballet and sat side by side in the center, in our front row seats. Muv had her favorite dancers and so did I, yet there was nothing to debate like when we attended the theater, here, we always sat in complete awe. However, on that particular night, I was watching Muv in the same way I absorbed the performance.

I was such a binary person and sat in judgment whereas she did not. I realized I had been judging her affair. She never sat in judgment when I gave birth. At times my mother seemed as old as the Nile and art was critical to her life, in the way it could elevate our lives and let the drama unfold on stage. Neither one of us appreciated the manufactured drama off stage and it was time to try and rise above it in the same way she was able to. She had taken me to the Geoffrey ballet when I was very young, then the theater, inspiring me, encouraging me to appreciate the arts and I had always been responsive, now I needed to respond by adapting a bit of her own attitude into my life.

I decided to let illusion and reality blend together. I could reconcile my dilemma by letting my previous life flow into my new one. On that night, the joy of watching the artists, including Muv, transferred itself onto my own feelings of being the product of a love affair. It was a fanciful idea yet it felt as real as the dancers on stage. I was different, and it was no longer a secret; I could embrace the truth and accept the new me.

London and we remained close friends. In the mid 90's he came to visit me in Seattle and I threw a party for him and invited half my family, when we were still on speaking terms. After Muv's confession I went to Europe with Francis for a couple of weeks and spent two days in London, and made sure to visit Liam. After a long chat he mentioned the party and said, as if offering a vital clue, "No wonder you had to work so hard with them."

His response was insightful. I had devoted so much energy apologizing to my siblings for my close relationship with Muv without knowing it.

The year 2000 allowed the next domino to fall, which included the tragic death of Blaine and the unfortunate circumstances surrounding it. Blaine and I had been very close, I never had to lift a finger to earn his affection; we adored one another. When I was a toddler I managed to find my way into a den with a wild boar. He jumped over the wooden fence without hesitating and rescued me. He probably saved my life. He loved to tease me because I was a constant source of entertainment for him. Whenever I walked into a room a sense of pride came over his face. He was nine years older and he treated me differently than the other siblings. He liked to introduce me to people and he taught me at the age of fourteen to always shake a person's hand when introduced. Then he became sick, and found Jesus Christ. Our relationship deteriorated quickly. I was never one to impose my way into another person's life if I felt any resistance, including Blaine.

When he was initially diagnosed with a brain tumor I stopped visiting him because I suspected he didn't want me to, then his conversion followed his illness, which only served to create more distance. The last time I saw him was at a family brunch in Seattle. When I started asking ques-

# 6

# HUMILIATION

2000

~

T he year 2000 proved easier to greet but I was still hungover from 1999. Muv's confession weighed less on my mind although it carried casualties. The most pressing issue was how quickly my relationship with my neighbors had become adversarial. I didn't agree with their endless lawsuit and knew we would lose the case again; which we did. I also suspected other lawsuits would follow and they did. Francis knew I wanted to move and we agreed the legal fees were making us feel hostage. House-boats were famous for being easy to sell and we decided we would put it on the market while I started looking at rentals. I wanted off that dock.

My biological reality became a story to share with close friends and the talk therapy became critical in letting the rest of the air out of the experience. A friend might say, "That took courage," or other reactions focused on the mother-daughter relationship. Until Liam heard my story. We had lived together when I studied at the University of

tions about his faith he became so angry and so fast, defensive of this fresh, deep emotional commitment to Christ. It was confusing at first until I understood; if I didn't feel the same emotional investment and didn't wish to engage in his religion, apparently I could no longer engage with him.

I considered my family benign. This would later feel naive after the in-laws enlarged our family. However, one fact remained constant; if religion played a role in our family, which it did, it was relaxed and rarely discussed. Blaine's conversion rattled me because of its intensity and how it transformed his personality. With five kids in our house, there were fights and arguments, but nothing dramatic. Some of us were artistic, others athletic and my middle brother kept to himself. We hadn't created problems in the neighborhood in our youth and my parents were well liked in the community. They enjoyed being involved in the church, it offered an opportunity to express their faith and engage with friends. My mother was the Director of Weddings and whenever the rare shotgun wedding came her way, Muv was able to engineer the event so that everyone's attention was taken away from the fact the bride was going to give birth at any moment. She could put a rococo twist on anything as if style was a sign of courage. My father sat on the Vestry but going to church was much more a social event than a religious occasion. For years we attended most Sundays, and we listened to a five-minute sermon, and sang a few hymns. But it was the social hour following the service that meant the most. We drank coffee and punch and ate cookies and caught up on Magnolia's gossip.

Muv, from the beginning, tried to be supportive of Blaine's marriage. She paid for their entire wedding, which turned out to be an expensive affair at her cousin's ranch in Northern California; many of our summer holidays were spent at this ranch and Muv was instrumental in making sure it was a seamless affair. Yet if she had any concerns about their marriage she kept them private. She honestly assumed everything would get better and her goal was to try and get along with Karen.

Blaine's conversion inspired me to start investigating the evangelical movement. My impression was that his wife used the religious movement as a lever to polarize the family. Norman had warned me the evangelicals often have their own agenda. Blaine's company sent him to Germany for a few months, but then his brain tumor returned and he and his family returned to their home in Tacoma, located south of Seattle. My parents were allowed two or three visits to see Blaine but for months news was not forthcoming. Then she received a phone call her son had died.

In the days following, I made a dramatic decision and called Muv. "I'm not going to the memorial service," I said. "She will find a way to humiliate you, and the family. Those evangelicals do things differently. I can't go to that event."

Muv was lost in her own thoughts. "I wondered if they might separate a few years ago, I went to see them once and there were shoes strewn about the front lawn as if they'd been thrown out the night before." She sighed. "But those three beautiful boys kept them together." Muv admired his faith, even if she was often taken back by the attitude and actions that came along with it. Muv finished our conversation by saying, "Karen took care of him and we have to go to the memorial service. It's your choice, I can't tell you what to do but I absolutely must go to my son's memorial service."

When I shared my decision with Francis he said, "It's an important ritual to participate in and say good-bye."

"I agree, but some of us won't be participating, we'll be

at the receiving end. I need to go sailing where I can mourn him on the water, in my own way."

Sailing offered a major channel of escape. Francis loved nothing more than an excuse to get on the boat. Weather permitting we went sailing every weekend and this time we ventured further up north. I wondered how much of Blaine's attitude had to do with the effects of a brain tumor. There was the tragedy and then there was the legacy.

I called Muv immediately after returning back to Seattle. She sounded distant, "It lasted for three hours, Bailey. There were so many speeches, I didn't even recognize the person they were talking about, as if having a tantrum in the office was funny. I guess I just didn't get it." I imagined her looking out across Puget Sound, hoping the view could take her away. "I think it was the hottest day recorded in August. Your father was taken to the hospital the next day." She hesitated as if she wasn't entirely convinced, "The doctors said it was exhaustion."

"Is he alright?" I asked. I had noticed my father was walking more slowly and staring at his feet, and his body had begun to hunch over. But this wasn't the time to bring up my theories about his dementia.

"He seems to have recovered, I think he's fine, he just went out to get some milk." She continued about the funeral, "Sally went around telling anyone who would listen that you'd gone sailing rather than attend Blaine's funeral. The entire event was..."

I intervened, "Well, that's probably the first time she's ever told the truth."

Muv continued, "I still can't believe it. She didn't put us in the front row, we sat behind people I didn't even know, as if we weren't family. Then it became gruesome, when I watched my son being put into the ground I thought I was going to faint. I looked around and suddenly there weren't any chairs, as if they'd been taken away, I could have sworn there were chairs, there were two of them right there. Then it was finally time for her speech. And you know what she said, 'We can only hope that Blaine's family finds Jesus Christ.'" Muv's voice had been so quiet until she began enunciating every word. "She was grinding her teeth as she said it, Bailey, when she suggested it was time for us to find Jesus Christ."

"Mother, I'm so sorry, that must have been just awful. Would you like me to come over now? I can be there in a minute."

There was a painfully long silence and I could practically hear her reliving Karen's final speech in her head. "Oh, I'm fine, I'll be just fine." Then her familiar voice came right back out of nowhere as she said, "Have a great day dear!"

And that's when I decided to take her to Italy.

# 7

# DEATH AND PRAYER IN POSITANO

~

Prior to Blaine's death I booked a ten-day cooking trip in Positano. Instead of meeting up with Francis somewhere on the continent I decided to extend it and take Muv to Europe for a month. I needed to put a pause in the family drama. I thought I could take her away from death and give her a vacation from grief. We spent ten days in Italy before driving up to Paris, then two days in London. It was time well spent together; our mother-daughter dynamic allowed us to become best of friends.

The first two weeks we stayed at a favorite hotel called Villa Franca hanging off a cliff overlooking the Mediterranean on the Amalfi Coast. Each morning I, along with eight fellow food enthusiasts, eagerly took notes at the home of our teacher, Diana Folonari. Her villa was within walking distance from the hotel. It also overlooked the sea and we couldn't believe our good fortune. After two hours of cutting vegetables and learning the art of 'Slow Food' we ate our lesson for lunch, and drank white wine.

Then I went down to the beach to find Muv. She was easy to locate because she often ate at the same place. I always found her enjoying her second or third cup of American black coffee while Italian waiters happily fawned over her. I doubt many tourist acted as grateful as Muv, indulging in a plate of pasta every day, sometimes both at lunch and dinner. After a lifetime of a relatively strict diet it was time to let it go. Everything was perfect and if it wasn't, she didn't complain because she rarely did.

We visited Pompeii and after our history lesson we silently concluded we'd had enough of death. Positano provided a kinder solution with heavy sun to give us cover. Our itinerary didn't deviate much because we were content to roam aimlessly around town, checking out the art and life on display. We bought books from local artists and lit candles in the churches.

Italy felt like a balm and each time we entered a church we took back our own interpretation of religion. Muv never lit a candle; sometimes there were dozens already flickering. In public she wore her religion as lightly as Italians often do in private. She watched me light candles, then she'd study the interiors, imbibing the glamorous traditions, replacing everything the evangelicals had managed to scrape out of the experience. The smells along with all the elegant pomp and ceremony fell back in place. During Blaine's illness I knew Muv often went to a large gothic Catholic Church on Capitol Hill.

Walking out of the dark ambiance into the bright Italian sun, Muv would casually say, "Maybe I should convert, they do it so well."

The majority of our time was spent walking up and down steps and gawking at the view. Each day ended the same way: after dinner we came back to the hotel, our refuge, to loiter over a glass of wine or a cup of coffee at the bar. It was a pleasure to retire to our voluminous bedroom with its high ceilings and whimsical floor covered in blue and yellow ceramic tiles. There were two double twin beds and a charming spacious balcony overlooking the bluest sea we'd ever seen.

No matter where she was, whether in Seattle, San Francisco, or Positano, Muv woke up early to allow plenty of time to properly put on her face and get dressed. It was the same process in reverse before getting into bed. She never deviated from this routine. When I was still small enough to sit on the bathroom counter with my feet in the sink, I found it hypnotic to watch her. We both studied her image in the mirror as she applied her make up. If her eyes caught mine they'd close slightly in her attempt to smile while putting on her lipstick. Even the small act of putting on lipstick seemed to have a purpose. I think her elaborate routine was a form of meditation in response to having five kids and multiple activities throughout the day. My parents spent a lifetime driving us from one event to the next. Once upon a time we must have been happy, of this I was convinced.

Never considered beautiful, in the classic sense, my mother was handsome and took care to keep everything that way for as long as possible. The first task was her teeth. Flossing was followed by a tiny rubber tool used to massage in between each tooth. Seated on the edge of the bathtub, lost in thought, one hand resting on her lap until it was time for the final brush. She stood up in front of the mirror, her three fingers applying Pond's Cold Cream with specific circular motions covering first her forehead as she pushed back her grey bangs, then face and neck. Sometimes her mouth would move as if repeating a piece of recent conversation. When she was satisfied with a personal edit she might say it out loud.

I felt like a kid again watching her swipe a tissue from the Kleenex box and glide by my bed onto the terrace. She stopped and surveyed the scene, each time like it was the first. Time was still on her side; I doubt she even knew how to waste it. My routine was a relatively quick affair and I was in bed, sitting up against the pillows reading a short story by David Sedaris out loud. The one about his brother who keeps sticking his tongue into the light socket in the classroom.

I have trouble finishing the story because I'm laughing so hard. "Can you believe that?" I gasp.

Muv responds straight away as if wanting to throw me the one thought on her mind. With a playful but direct gaze she emphasized each word, "Oh yes, you all had your own little quirks."

I stopped laughing because she left a cloud of serious-ness in her wake. She wanted lots of kids and got them. She enjoyed the noise, the activity, the distractions as long as she could carve out her own time, which she did. I closed the book and followed her out onto the terrace. The sun had set but there was plenty of light in the sky. I watched her figure motionless in front of the wrought iron balcony. Her hands on the railing, her palms relaxed, facing the sky, perhaps in prayer. My bed was next to the terrace, her profile in full view. I knew her thoughts were filled with her son. He's young and alive, and we're all full of quirks, and Muv is perfectly serene.

# 8

## THE MAN WHO CAME TO DINNER

~

Two months later Muv called me, "You're never going to guess who's coming to visit from Napa Valley."

"You're kidding. Victor's coming to Seattle? When?"

"They arrive on Thursday. Do you want to have them over for dinner on Friday? I think it can be arranged."

It was kind of her to ask, but I knew it was already decided. I had not spoken with Victor since Muv revealed his true relation to me. Furthermore, Victor had been Blaine's godfather. "They didn't come to that awful service, did they?"

Muv said quickly, "No."

"So, dinner for six?"

"Yes. Are you sure you're alright with this?"

"Of course I want to see him. Dinner here would be perfect. I found a rental house on Queen Anne, so this will be my last dinner party, my final supper."

Muv was genuinely curious, "Are you sure you want to move off the dock after that beautiful renovation."

"Yes, I'm positive, oh, and there's another lawsuit. Someone is suing the house in front of them because they want a better view. They want their neighbor to move his houseboat 12 inches to the left, or to the right, I can't recall."

The week came and went. My parents picked Victor and Carolyn up from the hotel and everyone arrived on time, and the company was quite civilized. This crowd wouldn't dare allow the tiniest slice of awkward silence to wind its way into our midst. Muv was happy to be with old friends, her personality more relaxed because they shared the same stories, as if they'd even brought their own oxygen from Northern California to Seattle.

Carolyn walked in, Californian to the core—the same long blonde hair worn loose. I focused on her first and gave her a glass of wine. She was relaxed and friendly, breezy and sexy. She and Muv spoke the same cosmopolitan language; whether or not they wanted to be in my home proved irrelevant. They were doing this for me, and I must tread lightly.

After I engaged with Carolyn it was time for Victor and we danced around one another; the boxer and his daughter locked in our little ring. Both off balance, we were hanging on the ropes under the gaze of others, unsure of everything but our DNA.

After drinks Victor sat down next to me and this seemed to be the closest we'd ever get other than an affectionate hand placed on the arm. For one fantastical moment I wanted to blurt out the obvious, like Muv had done. As recent as the affair appeared to me, it had been securely tucked away long ago, between old and dear friends, conspirators sharing the same ancient code. If I was also a co-conspirator there was no desire to hurt the people I loved the most. My father had recently lost a son and he didn't need to lose a daughter too. As I looked around the table I was acutely aware of the central issue; I had two fathers but only one had loved me like his own for my entire life.

*Why shouldn't he want to take full credit*, I thought, aware of his frail ego, he deserved it, which made the entire event feel bitter sweet. I couldn't help but compare the two men. Due to Blaine's death and my father's recent decline in health, he looked the same age as Victor who was a decade older. Both men were athletic but Victor had continued to train his mind and body. As much as Victor could make me laugh and feel at ease, for all his warmth and wit, the experience was destined to feel slightly superficial. We would have to wait to express our mutual affection and when we did it would be worth it.

I saw genuine affection between the two men, and I think my father respected Victor for his natural ability to hold everyone's attention and entertain. Victor was sensual, while my father was not, but they each trusted their instincts, and if those two could sit together throughout this meal with such ease, so could I. In the same way the night at the ballet let the illusion flow into reality, so did one father fall happily under the other's spell.

I suspected that everyone knew the secret and that everyone was here for my benefit. Victor was here to remove any mystery and to make himself available. The strange occasion did feel slightly anti-climactic because, like my biological daughter, I didn't have any expectations. But I was proud to be the boxer's daughter, and I was happy to know I could move on; it was the kind of night that sealed my future.

# 9

# THE FINAL DOMINO

~

The following month we moved off the dock and into the rental house on Queen Anne. It was an old bungalow with an expansive view of downtown, Puget Sound, the Cascades, including the village where I grew up. I could just barely make out our house buried behind the trees. Our furniture was cramped inside, and the place looked lopsided. When we walked upstairs to our small bedroom I was never sure whether I was walking up or down but I loved it and felt liberated from the houseboat community.

Our happiest times were spent on water. Our first boat was called *Papillon*, a 33 foot Nauticat. She was our training wheels. We decided to honor superstitions heavily prevalent in the sailing world by conducting an elaborate re-naming ceremony. At the time we still lived on the houseboat and *Papillon* sat along the length of our back porch. We invited a dozen friends, most of whom watched from the balcony above, amused, drinking wine and champagne while we threw salt and spice across the bow and read poems meant to appease the gods of wind, in particular Poseidon.

Early days aboard *Papillon* with Colette and Godot were ideal, and we explored dozens of destinations throughout the Pacific Northwest. The scenery was exceptional offering that rare navigable space where mountains and water unite. I was eager for short excursions and comfortable with destinations that didn't exceed a long weekend.

Being members of the Seattle Yacht Club meant we could take advantage of its reciprocity privileges. The club's social scene was casual, the restaurant quite good, and the wine list fantastic, but the ability to utilize other yacht club's facilities and dockage attracted us most. The reciprocals proved both economical and encouraged the travel itinerary to expand. SYC was exceptional at securing relationships locally and internationally. Over time we took advantage of reciprocity at San Francisco's Yacht Club, then Canada, Europe, and Asia.

*Madi* presented an entirely new proposition and required greater expertise. She was loaded with 30,000 pounds of teak and rigging, along with an engine that could carry enough diesel fuel to take us across an ocean. Francis suggested we get certified in bareboat sailing. *Madi* intimidated me because of her weight and we didn't have bow thrusters to help control her when maneuvering in and out of small spaces. I agreed to the class so off we went to the Caribbean for a two-week intensive course focusing mostly on navigation with some emphasis on engine maintenance and provisioning.

After soaking up an awful lot of hot sun it was time to take the big test and get certified. Francis passed with flying colors. Me? I wasn't given a score, instead I was pulled aside, not unlike the time Professor Dore pulled me aside during rehearsal at Seattle University. Captain Thomas looked me straight in the eye, his tone sincere, "Now Bailey, I want you to promise me something, please, never ever do any serious offshore sailing. Promise?"

It was easy to make such a promise. I genuinely liked Captain Thomas, we bonded instantly, probably because I didn't fit the typical profile of his students. There was never any danger of over estimating my abilities.

~

*...A Tuesday*

~

FRANCIS WAS at a Starbucks downtown on the morning of 9/11 and immediately came home. We stood in the kitchen and watched the planes hit the buildings on a small television set. Francis had worked at JP Morgan in Manhattan and said, "I walked through that building everyday for three years of my life." We stood there, stunned. We never left the kitchen that day. I put aside my Italian cuisine and took out my French cookbook written by Julia Child. We made Beef Bourguignon because it felt like the only thing that could soothe. My parents came over for dinner and the four of us huddled together, in shock, unsure of everything but the beef bourguignon. We went through two bottles of Chateauneuf du Pape hoping our emotions might find comfort in the heavy food and wine.

Initially I reacted the same way as everyone else: I cut out the American flag from the back page of the New York Times and taped it onto my office window. But my patriotism lessened as news and fear mongering increased and took over the media airways. A month later I didn't feel the same solidarity. Everyone kept insisting we feel some level of fear. I didn't agree, in fact, my reaction was the opposite; I wanted to embrace it and face it by confronting my own.

I sat down with Francis one night after dinner and said, "I think we should sail to Europe."

He had recently left Microsoft and his latest project had an end date. "Really, I'd love to take a long trip but I'm not sure you would."

"No," I said. "I mean let's move to Europe. Permanently."

# 10

## PREPARING TO SAIL AWAY

~

By the end of the week Francis and I had successfully sold the idea to one another and began making plans. We were equally excited but once I began sharing our grand adventure with friends I was surprised by their lack of enthusiasm.

Over lunch I shared my disappointment with Norman, "Why isn't anyone happy for us. Even at the Seattle Yacht Club we receive lukewarm responses, but then most sailors talk about it and don't actually do it."

Norman, as calm as ever said, "There's three reasons for this Bailey, we're supposed to keep safe after 9/11 and chasing that kind of adventure feels reckless. Secondly, the general mood dictates we tighten our belts and your trip sounds like you're being financially conspicuous. And thirdly, we're going to miss you."

I appreciated his clarity but it only served to bolster my attitude. I was insanely confident for two reasons; *Madi* was built specifically for this kind of trip and relocating full time felt keenly romantic. We had traveled to Europe several times in the last two years and I couldn't wait to bypass jet lag.

I started comparing my life to Dorothy in *The Wizard of Oz*. I convinced myself it wasn't by coincidence my city carried the nickname "The Emerald City." My emotional cyclone felt comparable to that of Dorothy Gale, even my little dog *Godot*'s name sounded eerily similar to Dorothy's companion *Toto*. Maybe I just wanted to channel Dorothy but if I ever landed in such a magical place, located 'over the rainbow', why in the world would I want to come back? I was still fond of the original series of children's books by Frank Oz and knew that Dorothy's mantra, 'There's no place like home' had been artificially incorporated into the movie. The original books insist Dorothy stayed in Oz and sent for her family later on. It didn't matter if this was all fiction because the fantasy of moving to Europe had a psychic pull so strong it convinced me the world was conspiring for it to happen.

It didn't even phase me that I failed a test and didn't have a 'Bareboat Sailing' certification in a little blue book. This would neither deter offshore ambitions nor dampen my enthusiasm. I simply chose to overlook any glaring deficiencies and considered them temporary obstacles to overcome. I decided if it wasn't for that unbearable Caribbean heat, I would have spent adequate time studying those tiny white sails and their positions on paper. I convinced myself that 'on the job' training would occur on the boat and this would have to suffice.

Of course this didn't erase my respect for Captain Thomas. He was highly competent. He transported dozens of vessels across the sea and he was the first person who came to mind when we decided to cross the Atlantic. Anyone attempting their first crossing, at least people like us, hired a captain, so I spent an entire weekend diligently combing through old contacts and phone numbers in the Caribbean trying to network my way back to Captain Thomas.

There was no such luck. Odds are he didn't want to be found. He was already burnt out by the time we took his course in the Caribbean, and his well weathered face spoke volumes. Even if I had managed to locate Captain Thomas he probably would have tried to talk me out of it. But once we committed to the adventure, the logistics took on a life of their own—they had legs and ran around occupying our minds day and night.

Francis, however, operated on a far more pragmatic level and did have concerns about leaving Seattle and all the security. Yet he never had any concerns about selling our stock options because neither one of us were the 'rest and vest' type. The golden handcuffs were meant to be cut off. Once the decision was made, it was easier to convince myself I would inherit my grandfather's passion for sailing on the trip. I also knew it would feel like hard work because this trip was not my fantasy; I was on a mission. I didn't want to play tourist in Europe anymore; I yearned to live on that continent permanently. Sitting on the deck outside our bungalow, looking out across Puget Sound, I envisioned my new life could offer the kind that was experienced on the wing of a dream. Every day I erased tiny fears by recalling how water had always played a part in my life. I was a strong swimmer, and there was nothing kinder on the eye and mind than getting lost scanning a large body of water.

My fantasies flew high while Francis tried to reign me

regarding the tedious realities of our future life. "You've no idea what a hassle it's going to be just to get a new driver's license."

These warnings flew right past me with such speed I could only catch up with their cruel meaning much later on. There was room for only one item to swirl around my head, and that was to get to the other side. It proved far more alluring than a task as monotonous as a trip to the DMV. Every day was packed with purpose. Francis was networking and trying to secure a permanent or consulting job across the pond. We made long, broad lists. They were then spun into intricate webs, each of us applying every ounce of our combined energy towards checking off every item.

Unfortunately, 9/11 made it impossible to sell our houseboat. I found a project management company to rent it out and take care of the particulars once we left Seattle. Francis took *Madi* up to Sidney to have her completely tricked out for her transatlantic voyage. Decisions arrived constantly with each carrying their own major significance. Sailors choose their model of boat with care, then decide whether or not to hire crew, or take their dogs, which route will suit their lifestyle and how to properly provision their vessel. Everyone had their own perspective but there's one item, perhaps the smallest, that received universal attention; the medical kit.

I had a good friend we fondly called Dr. Bob; he was a leading oncologist at Swedish Hospital. He was one of the finest and we trusted him implicitly. One Saturday morning we sat at his dining room table and he presented a document to impress; a compendium of everything that could possibly go wrong and how to fix it. He had typed up a lifetime of knowledge onto four 8 1/2 x 11 pieces of paper. The first time I went to the pharmacy I realized this list would need to be edited because there was only so much we could realistically store aboard *Madi*. Real estate is uniquely precious on a boat. But as with provisioning, each decision impacted our ability to survive. We did the best we could and this all became part of the adventure. Each sailor creates their own rules and it became surprisingly easy to commit because there's always another pressing item waiting impatiently to be addressed.

Then I was softly shocked to find each item had a confidently drawn X inside the box attached to it; except one. It was time to schedule the moving van and pack up our furniture, books, and my flying carpet. It would take much longer for the container to reach Europe than it would for us. I watched my former life drive away in a moving van. I took my last ferry from Seattle. I met Francis aboard *Madi* in Sidney. His choice of boatyard in British Columbia was based on economics; labor was cheaper and he could bypass sales tax. He had spent four months equipping the sailboat with new gear, including six new sails and a gorgeous spinnaker modeled after the Italian flag. He compared sails to gears and thought the overall effect offered greater steering power. A bow thruster would have helped *Madi*'s maneuverability but we had a budget and Francis stuck to it. We installed a new gen set, a water maker, re-did all the pipes with fiber glass to make sure nothing rusted, and changed the electrical fittings to adhere to European standards.

Later on, when the topic of the transatlantic voyage came up, I always asked Francis the same question, "Did I seem as scared as I was?"

His reply was the same, "No, you just wanted to get to the other side."

Truer words had never been spoken. It took months and

a million tasks to make our simple plan happen. We treated it like a military maneuver because it felt epic. There was no pause button. We maintained our focus which proved surprisingly easy because we were putting our lives on the line.

# 11

# WHEN TIME FELT FLUID

~

T his wasn't going to be a romantic cruise around the world. Francis had a job waiting in London and my goal was to get to the other side. Therefore we made an unconventional choice of taking the northern route. This meant a large section of the trip was spent driving and flying across Canada while *Madi* cruised over the Rockies on a flatbed truck. This was my favorite part—it was liberating to still be on land. I was in control yet released from the pressures of the city; home drifted further away even though we hadn't left the continent. We were on the move at last, with dozens of destinations propelling us forward.

Growing up in Seattle meant that both Vancouver and Whistler were regular destinations. They had become world class holiday spots, and we breezed through them, looking for adventure in the rest of Canada. This proved a unique treat because the country constantly exceeded expectations. Montreal and Quebec were cosmopolitan gems. With only

30 million residents in the country, Canada's cities seemed all the more exotic with so much space in between.

Then glitches became a way of life. The Canadian technicians in the boatyard took twice the time we anticipated to update *Madi*. By the time she was ready the truck was no longer available. The trucking company said they could transport the masts so we took them off and sailed without, safely, underneath numerous bridges stretching between Vancouver and our next port in Richmond. When the truck became available, we put *Madi* on the large flatbed so she could cruise over the mountains while we flew high above in an airplane with Colette and Godot.

We arrived in Pickering, Ontario, one week prior to *Madi*, however we encountered a major glitch. With just one mile left to go the trucker hadn't anticipated the low height of the last tunnel and *Madi* lost a starboard winch. She had to be repaired at the small boatyard in Pickering, and thankfully the task was completed on time and under budget. Time became more fleeting and precious than ever because with each glitch I felt we got further away from our schedule. We had chosen a route and a season when the weather was still on our side.

After the winch was repaired and the boat re-assembled, after re-setting the mast and re-tensioning the rigging, *Madi* was ready to go back into the water. After more complications with the launch, we finally got her floating again, and prepared to make way.

*...onshore*

FIRST WE SAILED to Kingston and met our captain. I probably chose him because his name was Tom. I had interviewed him over the phone because he lived in California and he convinced me of his nautical proficiency. I wasn't aware of his personal story. When we met at Kingston I was distracted by his dramatic hairstyle. He didn't have a hair out of place, and there was so much of it. The rusty colored shade of red looked unnatural until I finally figured out it was a head piece. Once the secret was out, he proceeded to tell me about his recent recovery from cancer, his divorce, and how he had lost all his money. I didn't ask but suspected this last bit was the reason he accepted our offer. In a car you can learn a lot about a person, but on a boat you learn everything.

We started navigating the St. Lawrence by cruising through the scenic Thousand Islands and motoring down to Cornwall. Our first major incident occurred right before entering the province of Quebec; *Madi* ran aground. It was a tricky place with complicated currents but a boat owner never forgets running aground because it can put an end to everything.

In fairness, I was on watch, but we were all awake on the upper deck before lunch. It was an awful moment. Francis quickly put on his underwater gear and went down to investigate. Thankfully, no damage was done—*Madi* was a strong boat and we always knew she could withstand more than we could. This was the prime reason for choosing a 43' Nauticat; a boat built by the Finns to handle the Baltic Sea.

More problematic, however, was that we didn't have the right chemistry with Tom. Our trip was all about new beginnings and he was understandably bitter about his recent past. When he started psychoanalyzing Colette and Godot it set my back teeth on edge. The issue had nothing to do with my dogs. I played with the idea he was giving us room to make our own mistakes, but this wasn't why we hired a captain. We were paying him to do a specific job and be proactive, not passive. His response to running aground was cavalier, as if he wasn't engaged with us or with his job, and he rarely offered advice. His attitude tapped into my own deep fears that I had suppressed for good reason. I assumed we could rely on someone else but he didn't instill confidence. For the first time I understood why people didn't hire a captain, or crew, wishing to rely on their own instincts. Everyone's attitude affects everyone else in close quarters, not to mention choices made on a boat. After another couple of incidents, I decided I had to let Tom go and fired him.

Francis wasn't on the boat at the time. He was out on an errand getting a replacement item and when he returned he took it in stride and perhaps wasn't all that surprised. But he told me I might want to find another solution, otherwise, it was just the two of us on one very big ocean. It wasn't my best move, being a dilettante, and sailing across the Atlantic was not my ideal mode of transportation; yet the problem was mine to address.

I trusted Francis and his ability to handle *Madi* completely. He knew every inch of her, especially after working shoulder to shoulder with the technicians in Sidney, but my level of competence was nowhere close. I was periodically reminded of the time Captain Thomas pulled me aside warning me about my lack of nautical knowledge.

However, what concerned me most was the lack of sleep. The notion of two people responsible for long watches, in charge of immediate decisions, reminded me of something my father once said: "You know how much I love you but when you don't get enough sleep I know it's time to get the gun."

I started dialing the Seattle Yacht Club and managed to find a woman who was a keen racer. Jane had no experience with offshore sailing but we needed crew. We negotiated the going rate and made plans to fly her from Seattle to Halifax.

*...the rogue wave*

FOR NOW, it was just Francis, myself, and Colette and Godot. We crossed into the Quebec province and it was like entering another country. Everything was French. Cruising down the Beauharnois Canal was breathtaking as we transited the Beauharnois locks, the biggest lock drop in the world. Water management is impressive, especially in small, contained spaces. I was happy. It was a small stretch full of fantastic highlights as we cruised into Montreal at peak season with the Jazz Festival in full swing.

My optimism returned. We were stationary for another week so I was able to recruit another sailor, a young man named Francois whom I met on the dock. His experience didn't extend beyond the lake but I was desperate to have two people on each six-hour watch. Francois was a sweet young man who preferred speaking French so we decided he would be on watch with Francis who knew French, while I would be on watch with Jane, the racer.

We went to Trois Rivieres, then Quebec where we spent a week enjoying the funny accents, history, and the fairy tale quality that went along with the city. The St. Lawrence was starting to feel more like the sea than a river as we headed towards Rimouski, then arrived in Sainte Madeliene, the northernmost point of our trip. From there we hopped off to the charming town of Gaspe where we spent a couple of days.

I was comfortable navigating *Madi* into tight spots at various marinas when there was plenty of light, such as in the morning or late afternoon. But the challenge came when we had to find a small space at night, when weather and currents came into play; it could be a nightmare. We opted for an overnight sail to get us to Prince Edward Island, Canada's oldest province, but the weather was terrible as we surfed into Summerside, rejoining English Canada. Suddenly I found myself hanging off another boat at 4am in the morning, desperately trying to avoid a crash, feet flailing in the air, trying to hold onto *Madi*. Our loud shouting alerted the couple to wake up and assist. They were awfully nice, taking it all in stride, sailors always assist others in need, but having bow thrusters would have been even better.

Onshore navigation was an informal affair. Each morning we set the course before taking off, and tracked it by writing hourly entries into the ship's log, documenting our position on paper. We were cruisers, not racers, and Francis often chose a tack that didn't require us to trim the sails constantly. This meant it took longer to cover the distance but it was a lot less hassle.

Most of the time the trip was scenic and all-consuming, and far too quickly we arrived at our last stop in Nova Scotia. We flew in the crew and spent two weeks provisioning the boat. Having an adequate food supply was critical along with anything that could break and needed to be replaced. It was the last time we'd see a store before the Azores. I was more than happy to stay busy because the rest of the time was spent waiting for the right time to begin our transatlantic voyage.

Then I encountered my worst nightmare and we hadn't even left the dock. One morning I decided to go for a stroll and take inventory of the other boats at the dock. I turned a corner and stopped dead in my tracks. My eyes were gripped by the sight of what was once a sailboat, but now a wrecked mess. The harder I stared the more I saw a portrait materialize before my eyes; this boat looked identical to *Madi*. It was as if I was seeing into the future when a catastrophe could strike and ruin everything. It was so overwhelming, I hardly noticed there was a man standing in the middle of the boat. I don't think he wanted to be seen, but I couldn't keep myself from asking:

"What happened?" My eyes kept sweeping his vessel.

He looked up at me wearily knowing I wasn't going anywhere. Then he said, as if it made all the sense in the world, "It was a rogue wave."

It was the first time I ever heard of a rogue wave but didn't dare follow up with another question because I wasn't sure I wanted to know the answer.

He limped towards me, "The Coast Guard saved our lives. My wife broke her leg, another broke both arms, we're just happy to be alive." Then he sighed, "But the dream is dead." He added unnecessary, "Obviously."

I stood there in disbelief. I was also relieved we'd bought a round of drinks for a couple of guys in the bar the previous night, knowing they were from the Coast Guard; that was just good etiquette. There was no need to continue the conversation but I wondered whether he had waited patiently for the correct time to depart. For the first time I kept my mouth shut. I felt deeply sorry for this stranger, and absolutely baffled there was any such thing as a 'rogue wave'.

I spent the next hour walking along the dock trying to replace that image. I tried to find comfort in the boats and became satisfied to find them intact, most without a scratch. By the time I returned to *Madi* our boat was empty and I found everyone having lunch at the marina.

When Francis greeted me he had a shiny look on his face, "Guess what, we leave tomorrow." He was beaming and I couldn't help join in with the others until the image of that boat crept back. In less than twenty-four hours we had to go; well, I thought, that's why we practice denial. Later that day I told Francis about the boat.

"Really," he said, "most sailors don't believe in rogue waves."

It was too late to contemplate whether or not he was allaying my fears. In any case, it was immaterial to him, as Francis had a completely different experience. He spent the previous night star gazing and said, "All the visible planets are properly aligned," as if this was all he needed to know. He was also half German. When he wasn't being Italian and romantic, he was as serious as a heart attack. For this I was grateful.

# 12

# WHEN TIME FELT EXPOSED

Offshore, or twenty-four-hour sailing, is a formal exercise. Someone needs to be awake and in charge at all times. The planning is far more intense with signed handoffs executed in the log. Position is noted hourly in the log along with weather conditions and additional notes. We engaged a weather service to call in for daily updates on our black satellite phone.

The first night began with a wonderful dinner. I prepared filet mignon with slices of avocado and a delightful raspberry vinaigrette dressing. Everyone appeared to enjoy it but after cleaning up the galley I noticed Francois had gone missing. I went to look for him and found him throwing up the entire meal over the railing. It was Francois's first time off the lake. I hoped the fish enjoyed it as much as the rest of us, and gave him some Dramamine to make him feel better.

The first ten days were deceptively calm and tranquil. There was plenty of room on the boat, the salon was spacious, with enough smaller areas for everyone to escape, and comfortable berths for our crew. We literally didn't change course for days, so keeping the sails trimmed and ensuring there was an appropriate amount of canvas was key. We experimented with sail configurations, and I learned more than when I took the class in the Caribbean, although from time to time I fantasized about having Captain Thomas on board. Francis decided, due to stiff breezes, the best for *Madi* was a Genoa-mizzen sail combination, as it balanced the boat and helped the autopilot stay on course.

We tried, as much as possible, to avoid using the engine for the crossing. *Madi* could motor over a thousand nautical miles on her tanks but we needed to cover at least that distance using sails alone or we could potentially run out of fuel. We also used the sat-phone to download weather markers onto our charts on a regular basis which helped us plan. Having worldwide chart software was a godsend.

It often felt like we spent more time chasing the wind than anything else. Most days came and went without much fuss and then the fun began. Every single day between four and five in the afternoon the dolphins came to play at our bow. First we'd see two, then twenty dolphins would arrive out of nowhere. We sat at the bow dangling our feet below the railings, watching them play and roll over, showing off their bellies. This lasted for about an hour until they set off to spread their joy elsewhere.

When we saw a whale everyone became so excited and took pictures. I found the sight both beautiful and terrifying as if that whale was the perfect metaphor for our trip. If I had wanted to go into the belly of the whale and face my fears, now I just wanted to run away yet there was nowhere to go. She was almost twice the size of our boat, floating about ten meters away.

The most magical aspect of the trip was the moon. I was

happiest on watch when I could escape for an hour to the aft deck, alone. Jane was married and raced boats, and those were the two items occupying her entire life. I didn't dare bring up the ballet or theater. Getting away was a luxury as I tucked myself under the large blanket, staring at the sky, amazed the moon could fill up the entire space. She barely left room for all the stars and there were so many of them. It changed my life without my knowing it. Later on I would crave that kind of nature on land, and for now, my senses remained on high alert.

At sea, there was always something to look out for, like debris or logs that fell off cargo vessels. For some reason this terrified me the most because they could do major damage very quickly, almost like the rogue wave. The relief of getting off watch at midnight promised sleep, but there was only so much Vicodin to take. I was thankful to Dr. Bob but I never was keen on pills. Still, sleep was always a challenge. Our berth was spacious and I craved my time alone, hoping for sleep. Unfortunately I often felt like a bottle of Coke in a dispensing machine, rolling back and forth, constantly.

The dogs never seemed stressed and the poop deck was easy to keep clean. Colette spent most of her time in a pouch around Francis's neck with Godot trying to avoid me on the bed. What Francois lacked in offshore experience he made up for in other ways. One time he and Francis spent six hours fixing a starboard light. Time took on another dimension.

Days passed without seeing another boat. At night if we caught one we'd quickly look it up in one of our manuals trying to count the lights, trying to figure her out, but it often remained mysterious. Everything remained mysterious except our sense of time because we were constantly monitoring it.

# 13

## A REPRIEVE, A SURPRISE

~

When we arrived at Lajes das Flores, the western part of the Azores, I kissed the ground several times. It was time to reward our efforts at successfully arriving at the midway point by getting drunk at the bar. This was particularly fun because I had opted to make *Madi* a dry boat, for no other reason than to underline the seriousness of our mission. There was the bottle of unopened scotch, that was mandatory on a boat, but it remained untouched until we were closer to our destination.

The following day Francis and I went for a long walk and strolled by these perfect little white stucco homes with their gardens full of pretty pink and red flowers, often enclosed by a charming white picket fence. I fantasized about staying, because this place felt perfect, we could live here. But we had to continue because that was our plan.

We stayed for a couple of days to catch up on our sleep then sailed to Horta and found one of the most colorful marinas in the world. Horta was the essential stopover for sailors, she even provided a specific space for each sailor to leave their mark, literally, by painting their own mural with pastel crayons. Which we did, of course. I doubt Horta was open to commercial vessels and the spirit of fanciful and romantic sailors was like surround-sound. I was of two minds. I engaged in the merriment and I wanted to get to the other side. We met plenty of eccentric sailors, like a German guy named Clemens who seemed perpetually stoned. He grew pot on his boat and it's safe to say his small garden acted as a medical kit. We met sailors who didn't even have a map. Two guys from Quebec were intent on crossing with just a compass and a bottle of whiskey. This made me laugh and feel all the more grateful for our elec-tronic global charts. I didn't have their free spirit but I did feel the essence of success.

Our sat-phone made it possible to call Muv every couple of days, letting her know we were fine and on our way. Then I made the mistake of checking my messages. Suddenly, in the midst of the North Atlantic, a voice came through my phone that I hadn't heard in well over a decade. It was Steve, the man with whom I had the child, and gave up for adop-tion. I had made up my mind long ago that I would never interfere with her life, but he felt differently. Steve and I had gone our separate ways after her birth, and though I harbored no hard feelings toward him, we were no longer in touch.

His message caught me off guard; I hadn't heard his voice for so long and never dreamed of receiving this call and yet my senses were on such high alert I could almost forecast the entire conversation. The minute I heard his eager voice, I knew he had located our biological daughter. Our worlds were so far apart it made me wonder how he found my cell phone number. He wasn't the brightest guy and I wondered whether illegal means were used to obtain contact information. I saved the message and sat there on the boat imagining him sitting in front of the television watching an episode of Oprah about father's rights. I decided I must confirm suspicions if only to put a stop to any of his delusions.

I called him and tried to navigate the imaginary eggshells beneath my feet. Immediately he said, "I found her, her name is Heidi and she looks exactly like you."

That was a nice touch, but I remained skeptical. "Oh really," I said, and let him continue as the significance of her name sank in.

"I met her Dad and he's a preacher and I think her mother is a guidance counselor in a small town in Vancouver, Washington."

I laughed to myself. They were probably evangelicals. They even gave her a name to make sure she never forgot. Steve was eager with the details and I could just imagine how well he'd been managed during their meeting. I felt sorry for him and was deeply uncomfortable knowing it was critical to put someone in between us. I could practically hear fantasies of our becoming a family swirling around in his mind.

I said, "I'm happy for you, Steve, but to be honest, I'm calling you from the middle of the Atlantic. I'm moving to Europe with my husband, but listen, I'm happy for you. I'm calling from a satellite phone, I can't talk long, I really need to go."

Initially I was mad about his intervention. My future floated further away until I decided to call Tina, a friend from the past who shared our dorm room. Tina knew Steve, she had been with me before and after the birth. I gave her

Steve's number and knew she could pry more information out of him, more than I ever could. Heidi's family had met Steve and they must have drawn several conclusions on their own. This made me desperately sad. Thankfully I didn't have the bandwidth to dwell on it. It felt like a farce as my mind transitioned towards our next home.

# 14

# I DON'T THINK WE'RE IN KANSAS ANYMORE

*...the horror*

∿

We safely reached another island, the capital of the Azores called Ponta Delgada. It was the land of homegrown European pineapples and boasted the best mineral water we ever tasted. It was also time to say good-bye to one of our crew. Francois flew home which left the three of us to navigate our way to Gibraltar for the final ten days of our adventure. Unfortunately our good luck departed along with Francois. The weather changed dramatically. It was like a bankruptcy because it was so gradual at first and became life-threatening overnight. The waves were immense and flew over *Madi*. They became more dangerous by the hour as the water started seeping in through the windows. *Madi* was thrown about like a little cork in the middle of nowhere. All that was visible was water thrashing against us on all sides. The only option was to hang on and hope for the best. We just had the storm sail and mizzen up, and bullied through on the engine.

The poop deck was officially closed but no one drank or ate or needed to use the heads, we just sat in the salon periodically looking at one another for relief. There wasn't much and the salon seemed to shrink in around us. I was terrified and couldn't believe this was my idea as I held onto Colette and Godot trying to keep them from breaking their little bones.

For three days we diligently called in our coordinates, alerting the system of current weather conditions. Navigation was no longer possible. The problem with trying to get information is that if someone hasn't sailed through your area there's little information to obtain; you just have to hang on. It became a living hell. We had to wait until the weather subsided and the wind died down and we made landfall and refuge in the Port of Vilamoura in Portugal.

Once again I kissed the ground, over and over again. We sailed for another few days and the only thing I recall is the moment Francis finally announced, "We have found land."

There was the moon and there was that moment. We arrived at our destination in Gibraltar and docked at Sheppards marina, then said goodbye to Jane as she flew home. Then we found out the job offer in London was no longer available. It was time for plan B; unfortunately, we didn't have one.

*...time for something completely different*

GIBRALTAR BOASTED SO much sun yet the impression was stark. There were too few gentle areas to rest the eyes, except the water, but I was done with all that; it was land I craved along with a safe harbor where I could recover and engage in conversation. It appeared that most of the harbor's residents operated in the import or export business, yet I didn't think it was a good idea to obtain specific details. Sheppards was our new home, at least for a few weeks, but it didn't resemble any marinas I'd ever stayed on. The people were friendly and most were live-aboard. It was far from upscale and full of characters mostly living off the grid.

Francis found it immensely entertaining. I found it completely foreign. Our new home was at the nexus of Maltese, Moroccan, English, and Spanish souls congregating under their own rules. There was a Danish craftsmen who had lost several of his fingers. I spent some time with a woman who was the product of one of those children asylums illustrated in the movie, *The Magdalene Sisters*. It was a brave new world full of characters far removed from any network I'd ever known. The general layout of Gibraltar appeared scruffy and underdeveloped. The local politics were intense between the English and Spanish, and it was hard to understand or maybe I didn't want to make it my business because I thought our temporary home was a pit stop. If Gibraltar wasn't stylish, it was authentic, full of strong feelings which carried the aura of a small town in England—working class, bold, and often slightly jarring.

Without the job in London, fate was at play. Francis spoke several languages, unfortunately I spoke only one. We bought an old Mercedes, the kind of vehicle that could be discarded in a few months. She was the opposite of the fashionable sleek black model we owned back in Seattle. She must have been white at one time, but was now full of dings and dents. She had not only seen better days, but was on her last set of wheels. We named her Berta. Few parts worked, some critical, like the gas gage, and her roof leaked. But the engine stayed dry and reliable, and that was all we needed.

It was still summer so we crossed our fingers and threw a few suitcases in Berta along with a couple of towels across the front seats. Unfortunately it rained in Spain, so the trip from Madrid to Barcelona made me feel like we were back on the boat. We had family in France so we drove through the Carcassonnes and then stayed with our in-laws near Cannes until it was time to get out of their way. Our destination was a family flat located on Lake Garda in northern Italy. We would leave the boat in Gibraltar and take up residence at the unoccupied flat on Lake Garda, which turned out to be as pretty as any place I had ever seen.

It was beautiful and an adventure, but I didn't connect with my new identity as an ex-pat yet—nothing felt familiar. We were heading towards our future, not our past. At times we channeled Audrey Hepburn and Albert Finney in *Two For The Road*. It was the funkiest time of our lives. When Francis called one of his sister's on the phone she said, "Now the hard part, right?" I might agree if I hadn't just spent the last eighteen days crossing the Atlantic.

# 15

# ROME: WHEN TIME STOOD STILL
## 2002-2005

~

Lake Garda would remain our home away from home for years to come but it was too small for our furniture and we needed to find a place to call our own. From the moment we arrived in the Eternal City it felt like sensory overload, a feeling that penetrated my psyche for three luxurious years. Rome remained our favorite city even if she proved emotionally exhausting every now and then. It was best to start out early, when the bread was fresh and the stores were guaranteed to be open, before the long Roman lunch took over the day. The simple act of a morning walk could feel extreme. Even before I had crossed Piazza San Cosimato I could get sidetracked by a miniature opera unfolding across the street. I could be distracted by a young woman walking close by talking on her cell phone, suddenly bursting into tears, contemplating the futility of her life with hands slicing through the air, her Italian sign language in full swing. I couldn't look away and by the time she turned the corner she was laughing as if nothing had happened; the emotional spectrum covered in less than two minutes.

What really blew my mind was Rome's sense of time. As if it stopped and never shifted into the present. And I wasn't alone. When friends came to visit they were either convinced they must have been a Roman soldier in a previous life or they agreed with me; time stood still. This didn't effect the older residents. Change happened everywhere but here and they weren't remotely concerned; Rome would always remain eternal, mythic, and grand. These were the weariest people I ever met. My own expectations were vague because I couldn't believe we landed in Rome in the first place. Francis was convinced it was my idea and I was emphatic it was his decision. I no longer trusted my ideas after sailing across a large ocean. What we did agree on was landing somewhere that celebrated our grand transatlantic voyage; Rome was such a city.

Francis spoke the language and loved the dialect, but his family was from the northern border of Italy to France. Italy may be considered one country by others, but from within there are 20 separate countries with their own specific cultures. I often heard a well-worn phrase, "One may work up north but they live down south," and sometimes you hear Northern Italians refer to southerners as 'Arab' and southerners refer to the upper side as 'German'. In spite of it all, they're convinced of being Italian.

I had one concern and that was making sure our container eventually arrived in Rome. My first lesson was patience. Italy didn't believe in centralization. Each region operated autonomously, regarding everything, even their tax structure, as separate, and each came equipped with a unique attitude of distrust towards their government. This only served to exacerbate the awful bureaucracy and I'm convinced every single citizen could teach their own master-class in the art of patience.

We found a furnished apartment along Via Flaminia, the ancient road that begins at Porto del Popolo, at Piazza del Popolo. When Francis arrived from a business trip up north he always called me from this piazza alerting me it was time to put on the pasta. By the time he walked through the front door dinner was on the table.

When I heard the Italians would be protesting the Iraq war in 2003, I went on the march and walked through at least seven piazzas, keeping pace with the band as they belt out John Lennon's 'Give Peace a Chance' over and over again. The number of people was estimated at seven million. Politics aside, these people had a gift for hanging out and it was easy to get swept up in their energy. When I went home and turned on the Italian news it offered noth-ing. The Italians never forgot how the CIA kidnapped, and then later killed one of their most beloved Prime Ministers, Aldo Moro. Protestors were left alone in Rome and else-where, but Berlusconi kept it quiet on the world stage.

Trastevere

THE FLAT ON Via Flaminia wasn't special but the high ceil-ings were unforgettable. Its location was ideal and distracted me for several months until our container arrived. I needed to find a permanent home and roamed the city aimlessly, open to anything, until I walked across the Tiber and landed on the west bank. The ground shifted and I fell so deeply in love I knew we had to live right there. It took me a month to

learn how to pronounce 'Trastevere' but that didn't matter,
she was the most beloved district with a name to reflect it; in
Roman dialect they called Trastevere the "Cor di Roma". In
a town packed with 500 churches, one of the oldest and
most charming was located a few blocks from our new
home, it was called Basilica Santa Maria di Trastevere; the
entire neighborhood felt like a fantasy.

Then came the daunting task of unpacking 200 boxes;
but it was a happy task. It wasn't so much missing my stuff
as it was about surrounding myself with familiar items in a
foreign place. Once the magic carpet was unrolled, every
object found a place as if on its own. Our flat sat on the first
floor, or what they call 'primo piano,' in a classical building
covered in soft coral pink located on Via Angelo Tittoni.

Each week I walked around the corner and climbed a
series of steps taking me to the top of the Gianicolo or
Janiculum which made everyone feel like they stood at the
top of the city. The Gianicolo wasn't one of her famous
seven hills because it didn't need the attention, not with
those sweeping views and the serene Fontana dell'Acqua
Paola. Further along, there's the church where St. Peter's
crucifixion occurred and then the grand monument glori-
fying Garibaldi with his wife Anita close by; she was also on
horseback but carried a baby in her arms. Garibaldi lorded
over everything but the Vatican because he thought the
priests were a cancer on the country. This was his perspective and many northerners still like to perceive a country
that was never unified. To many, including Francis,
Garibaldi was a hero above all others.

After Garibaldi's statue, the Vatican was close by, which
proved convenient because friends might request I stop by
and say a prayer if a family member or friend was sick; if
time stopped here, Rome was still felt beyond her walls.

But most of the time I preferred the other direction. On a regular basis Colette and Godot were taken past the American Academy where I fantasized Gore Vidal was studying at the library doing research for *Julien*. This weekly sojourn took us to the seventeenth century Villa Pamphili located in the quarter of Monteverde. This is where Via Aurelia begins with her dramatically high, dark grey walls stretching up to the sky until a tiny world opened up for us alone. We'd enter the gardens and stroll by the pitch where Italians kicked a soccer ball around with their kids or Indians played cricket.

Villa Pamphili is one of Rome's largest landscaped parks but I felt destined to roam far beyond the manicured bits, below the glamorous gardens and gazeboes. Once we reached the shady area where dozens of giant pine trees with extra long trunks provided shelter from the heat, I let Colette and Godot off their leads. There were numerous paths and I took a less traveled one to our secret garden. I never saw anyone here. We were surrounded by headless statues, or women in repose on low beds of ancient marble, forgotten long ago. It was so quiet. Everyone appeared to have gone to sleep leaving the air clean and serene. I might meditate on my biological bookends, Victor and Heidi, for a few minutes, or how this ancient city could fit into my future. The statues might come alive, and we'd have a silent chat without words getting in the way. Rome had her own flamboyant past and this is where I could contemplate my own.

If I craved escape, Rome offered it in various shades of ochre. The more the paint peeled, the prettier she looked, ancient and romantic and completely undisturbed. Eventually I had my motorcycle shipped from Seattle to Rome, a little Honda 250cc Rebel. The police never bothered me even though she wasn't registered. When they saw the Washington license they might have assumed it carried diplomatic privileges, or more likely, the Roman Carabinieri or Polizia just didn't care. That small moto offered the most thrilling experience; driving her around the city, underneath the Sycamore trees along the river, weaving in and out of traffic. The trick was to relax, stay simultaneously aware of everything and ignore the rules.

Invariably I got lost but it was easy to find the Coliseum. It became a test. I tried to pretend the monument was familiar, like a tree I'd seen in our backyard since childhood, or a precious piece of furniture passed down from one generation to the next. It was a pointless fantasy and I could never imagine setting roots down or getting a job in Rome.

The few opportunities available for expats were found working for the FCO, one of the universities, or as a tour guide. I didn't have the credentials for the first two and lacked the desire to guide people around town. Luckily I could still live off my small consulting company in Seattle. After a lifetime of productive behavior, I was starting to drift which was easy because the summers were so hot. My moto offered the best means of escape; I'd put a light shift over my bathing suit and by the time I arrived at Ostia my legs were bronzed.

Francis and two friends had sailed *Madi* from Gibraltar to Rome so it was now my job to check on her every once in a while. Francis was busy shuffling between Rome and a consulting assignment up north near Milan. I'd cruise along the Tiber, then a half hour later I was at the beach. I'd check on *Madi*, take a short swim and dry off walking along the boardwalk. Back in the city I never knew where I was going but the detours took me everyplace I needed to see, the Baths of Caracalla, to Piazza del Popolo, and then the Coliseum, of course, which meant home was just across the river.

Then Pope John Paul II became ill. This changed everything and gave me a focal point. In the month of March, 2005, I stopped drifting and broke through the luxuriously stagnate environs of Rome. It encouraged me to make a dramatic decision regarding a personal conundrum. I had kept Tina's email full of Heidi's personal information but didn't pursue it. I wasn't about to break my cardinal rule about disrupting her life; I had already done enough damage. But recently I had stumbled back across the email. Tina was adopted and her email assumed her mother's predicament could be similar to my own experience. She had made contact with her mother; why shouldn't I?

# 16

# A PEACEFUL PILGRIMAGE

~

Everyone felt the gravity of the announcement. The Pope was dying and I lived just minutes from the epicenter. History's most well-traveled Pope and first non-Italian to hold the title of Bishop since the sixteenth century was allowing the Eternal City to unify the past and present. Italians won't react unless they have to do it in a minute. They prefer to turn on a dime after reducing one another to tears. That's how her non-residents are made to feel; it's a right of passage. The locals have to experience it so why shouldn't we? Yet they have the edge, weighed down by history and now it was unfolding in real time. It felt epic. I had to get in on the performance.

I started walking up the Gianicolo and down to the Vatican on a daily basis. In the early stages, the media were all kept at a safe distance from the piazza, our space was still sacred. The religious and curious pilgrims had yet to descend from all corners of the planet. For the time being, it was just me and the locals roaming around the ancient

Egyptian obelisk. We were acutely aware of the impending drama; like the calm before the storm. Some of us stood along the periphery beneath the colonnade, then we'd find our way to the forecourt, where we could look up at the Papal apartments. We were told the lights stayed on while he was alive. We kept vigil.

Then the lights went dark. The Pope was gone. I was triggered.

If I remained in limbo, history unfolded around me, and fast. Present time had finally arrived in the Eternal City, it was picking up speed and kicking into fourth gear. The media moved in unmercifully. It was insane and took such little effort to put aside tedious particulars and household duties. Francis was traveling and I didn't feel the need to track him down and discuss business bulletins. It was time to go native and channel the attitude of the Italian. The city was languid no more and it was time to pay homage. I watched as the media set up 'mobile homes', one after the other around the piazza. Within two days the place was packed and I took advantage of the situation. I talked with strangers and flirted with the usual suspects from Sky News, CNN, Fox, and all the rest. I watched the television personalities preen from their four-foot platforms, every once in a while they'd look down from their perch, smile, even engage for a couple minutes before happily returning to themselves and fussing with their make-up.

I didn't have a fixed destination, but there was an invisible guide whispering in my ear, leading me to believe even within this dark, postmodern world full of vulgarity and glaring wannabes, I was here with the rest of the world because the Pope had left the building. A man who opposed the war in Iraq, a man of peace; a man full of contradictions. Living in lock step with Catholic culture served to rekindle my Jesuit education including Chaucer's literary satire. Even if I didn't know Giovanni Boccaccio had written the original pilgrimage 300 years before, I was going to experience a pilgrimage, Italian style.

I had no intention of getting in the line on that day. I was adrift, confused as to whether or not make contact with my daughter, the clock ticking half past noon. Then I wandered into the end of the line without noticing it because Italians are often allergic to organization. However, there was never any doubt everything was under complete control. Not a uniform in sight. Italians have dealt with the Mafia; forever trained, they know how to blend in better than the Russians.

Slowly I became determined to brave this time-intensive, often suffocating adventure. I was going to see the recently deceased Pope. For twelve hours I was pushed by tiny Indian nuns while tripping over hundreds of empty plastic water bottles. We navigated around small European cars parked along the route, grateful to break the monotony by speaking with Italian 'nanas', these widowers or religious spinsters, as they leaned out of their 'primo piano' apartments. They complained about their confinement due to the zoo of humanity swimming beneath their windows. They whined as Italians are wont to do, in large dose and good spirit, their weariness intact, wearing a peaceful smile across their face. This was a special day for them, a special day for millions of people all around the world, including me.

At one point, just after I'd joined the line, I looked up and found a tall, striking man standing next to me; his name was Christopher and he would become my best friend for the next twelve hours. He was exhausted and very hung over. He'd taken a taxi directly from Fiumicino Airport. He'd flown first class and complained in typically obnoxious New

York fashion about the boring broad seated next to him. Christopher and I bonded immediately. He kept saying he couldn't have done this without me. I felt the same way. Just minutes before meeting me he'd anxiously looked for an escape route. He was handsome, older, wispy, slightly tweedy with a shock of white hair and bright blue eyes.

We shared a million stories, pieces of personal fiction, our opinions were like breathing. Our goal was to keep one another entertained. His father had been Chief of Police in the big apple so his gossip was full of the glamorous Kennedy clan and Sinatra. I told him my mother had seen Jackie at a museum in New York, struck by how large her face appeared, uniquely pretty and photogenic.

Christopher responded by saying, "I used to see her on the street, Jackie was all hair."

His father had taken care of Marilyn Monroe's New York apartment upon her death. Christopher had asked his father the same question we all had, was it murder or suicide? He looked at his son, "We'll never know." All his stories were full of nostalgic glory. Christopher had worked at TWA. He gossiped about Elizabeth Taylor and Richard Burton during their heyday on transatlantic flights. They were notoriously heavy drinkers, always seated strategically apart in custom made chairs, allowing them to comfortably fling drinks and expletives at one another in equal dose, colorful dialogue that lasted for hours.

One of Christopher's duties was to escort VIPs to their chartered planes and Pope John Paul II had been a client when he visited New York in the 70's. He was so moved by that experience he felt compelled to spontaneously board the plane just hours after hearing the news. This is why he was here, hung over, with me. I shared my predicament and why I was in line, he offered his perspective and indulged in personal frustrations; he felt like a minority in his city and emotionally irritated, as if New York was playing down the historic event. Even if he no longer practiced Catholicism, Christopher still attended the high Episcopal church of St. Thomas in Manhattan. Everyone felt triggered in their own way.

By the time the fifth hour arrived our exchanges became increasingly personal. He spoke of his Aunt, an Aunty Mame kind of figure in his life, who'd once said, "There are two people in this world, the lifters and the leaners. Get rid of the leaners."

He looked at me and said, "Bailey, thank God, you are a lifter!" He couldn't believe he was waiting in line and for so long; as a privileged New Yorker he'd never waited for anything his entire life.

Entering the ninth hour, after several respectful silences exchanged with nuns, after brief conversations with college students and tourists, the humor turned macabre. Every time the line lurched forward we were forced to run for a few minutes. It was like pressure released after untying a knot. Christopher started throwing out one liners like, "OK, Bailey, now listen, we're not really going to see the corpse, they're sending us to the gas chambers, one line for work, one line to be gassed."

His best friend was Jewish and they bantered constantly, nothing was too sacred and yet everything felt sacred between us. Small talk, or 'weather talk' wasn't our style as we consciously decided to make this peaceful pilgrimage lively and bearable for one another. It was psychologically difficult at times because the official estimating wait time was only four hours.

By the time we entered the Vatican, we were talked out and completely punch drunk. It was just minutes before midnight. Our relationship had completed its cycle with our loves, our selective prejudices, our mad impressions and personal philosophies. There was nothing left to say.

Upon entering the darkly lit Vatican we stopped talking and walked to the end in silence. We stared quietly at the Pope; diminutive yet profound in his remains. For a fleeting second it seemed wrong to take a picture until it became so easy to justify. It's exactly what Papa dictated all along, being a media savvy man, wisely perceiving each personal photograph taken would leave a far greater impression than any photo seen on the cover of a magazine. The Pope used his death as if it was the greatest recruiting tool. I had less than ten seconds to snap a picture and pay my respects, to view a blessed man, his face gray, slightly pained lay at one end with two very elegant red shoes famously designed by Prada at the other. He was so small as he lay but two feet away.

The lack of security would have felt alarming if we hadn't felt so safe the entire time. The security was invisible in a city full of invisible secrets. As with the Italians, it's always what they don't say that's most important. Christopher was baffled because he was convinced New Yorkers would have yelled and behaved badly. He didn't understand the tolerant atmosphere. I tried to convey, as an outsider, the cultural reality of the Italian mentality. That's why the spontaneous clapping, on the hour, this created a way to celebrate and release the tension at the same time. Along with the fact they just loved to hang out.

We stood outside the Vatican and talked about meeting for coffee the next day, and that was the last time I saw Christopher. I spent the next few days composing a letter to my daughter, including pictures and a past that didn't necessarily lend to a typical profile of a young woman in denial of a pregnancy. Or did it? Nothing felt typical after that day.

I called her number and the mother answered. As I predicted she remained in complete control of the situation. She came as advertised, to my ears, on guard and so nice and full of promises. I asked if I could send the package and letter. I said, "I just want her to have a little box she can take out of the closet and visit every now and then."

I spoke with Heidi for a brief moment and then her mother quickly got back on the phone. It was as it was; a beginning. If she felt curious she could take it out and read all about it. It felt like the right thing to do. Maybe she could be familiar with her DNA, even a little proud; I certainly was.

# 17

# CARAVAGGIO AND ALL THE REST

~

In winter a month of Saturdays were spent mining the magic of Michelangelo Merisi da Caravaggio; he who created blood and passion on canvas. It became a treasure hunt locating the various Caravaggio's strewn throughout Rome's churches and public buildings. The painter retained his ability to shock, and he lives in Rome, the way fashion lives and breathes in Paris and Milan. Caravaggio must have blown the mind of believers as he conveyed epiphanies most had only heard about in church.

Winter was also the season for puntarelle; a chicory flavored salad with white stalks carefully prepared and placed in ice cold water to remove any bitterness. This is a favorite dish in winter and it is divine. Francis brought cousins or business partners down to Rome every now and then, and they always congregated in the kitchen. They hovered over the stove discussing how important it was for pasta to be al dente, how it heightened the vitamins effectiveness, and why a specific amount of olive oil could trap heat into the water. They approved of my recipe for puntarelle, apparently I added just the right amount of anchovy, garlic, and pepper into the mix. I was relieved.

Roman men were easy to read but feminine cues much harder to decipher. If a man looks your way, a smile often follows; they flirt like they breathe. But when a woman finds you remotely interesting her eyes might rest for a while, then begin to resemble a glare. They're just taking inventory, or mentally taking down a couple of notes to file away for another day.

I never applied so much imagination to my ensemble; these women were in a class all their own. But I think it was often a reaction to the Pope, this style of hooker chic; it was both funny and fantastic. If I wanted to catch the fashion extravaganza one of the best places was along Via del Corso, preferably on a spring, Sunday afternoon. When they closed the street to traffic and opened it to every egoist wishing to parade up and down, until they meandered up the side streets to sit along the cafes at Piazza del Popolo or have lunch along the alleys leading up to Piazza di Spagna.

If you paid too much for your meal you weren't eating at the right place in Rome. It was meant to be affordable and when I wanted to extend the night I went to a funky bar with my gay friends in Trastevere. I became friends with an Irishman named Dermott who owned an English book store, an easy target if you wanted to meet fellow English speaking expats.

I felt like an outsider but then so did everyone else. The Italians don't even have a word for foreigner because anyone who didn't grow up in their part of town is called a *straniero*. I made friends with one Romana di Roma, a stunning woman named Carola Vannini who was biding her time teaching Italian to people like me until her home design career took off, which it did. I got along with my neighbors, one in particular, a young man named Roberto Purvis, who was a working actor and spoke at least eight languages. We had a small terrace outside our back door and his apartment was located above and sometimes he stuck his gorgeous face outside his tiny bathroom window and we'd have a chat.

Then there's the three-hour lunch to which everyone succumbs eventually. The Italians have many names for their eating establishments; pizzeria, osteria, trattoria, enoteca, pizza al taglio, ristorante—but once you've landed at your favorite joint you'll want to stretch it out in Rome. After the second or third course, waiters simply put the bottle of mirto or limoncello at the table and left us to it. Seeing Susan Sontag at the forum had a surreal effect and watching the ballet at the Baths of Caracalla in the open air was a night I never forgot.

Rome was a place to drift and I did and then Muv became ill for the first time. I flew home and nursed her back to health over ten days, or so she said. After a lifetime of perfect health her blood cell count became difficult to manage. By the time I left, she was fine and a few months later I made plans for them to come visit for a month.

I took her to the Vatican for a Christmas Eve service and it was awfully kind of Pope Ratzinger to walk right in front of us in the middle of it; Muv was captivated. My father wasn't doing very well and Rome overwhelmed him. It wasn't that I couldn't get him out of the apartment; I couldn't get him out of the chair. It was alarming and he finally admitted there was a problem. What it was we weren't sure but I was certain it was linked to dementia; and I was proved right on my next trip to Seattle. I went back to the west coast, like clockwork, every six months but it was stressful trying to see friends and find new clients. I only went for ten days at a time and even that was beginning to feel like too much.

Francis had started a company in Malta. He decided to invest most of our money into an IT startup and gradually began spending more time in the middle of the Mediterranean. I visited him a few times but didn't like Malta, apparently he was growing to love it enough for the both of us. My reaction to his devotion towards the island was to take an overnight train with Colette and Godot to Paris. The more time Francis spent in Malta, the more I fantasized about moving to Paris.

Then one day in late summer I was walking home after an extended lunch with friends. Rome felt heavier than usual. It was hot, and it reminded me of that one summer in 2004, when all of Europe was on fire. Rome experienced temperatures around 100 degrees for almost four months. I loved Rome but I hated the heat. I was thinking about Francis spending all that time in Malta, another excruciatingly hot place, I could practically feel his dominant attitude trying to pull me where I didn't want to go.

I walked through Piazza San Cosimato and didn't want to look up; I knew the sun was at the highest so I stopped and listened as the church bells rang. It was always so beautiful yet on this day the sound was too loud. When they stopped it was almost deafening. I looked up to the balconies on either side and there wasn't a person to be seen or a voice to be heard.

It made me think of my own voice, I could practically hear it saying, "This is not your city and it never will be." It sounded almost ghoulish as I walked the last block to our home on Via Angelo Tittoni. The following week I took another overnight train to Paris with Colette and Godot.

This time I started meeting with real estate agents, and then I found the perfect flat.

~

## Arrivederci

~

IT WASN'T A SIMPLE DECISION. It was hard to understand how a city so dearly loved could inspire me to leave it. I lifted the small, wrought-iron chair from across the little table and moved it so I could stretch my legs out. I wanted to look at the monument and try and remember all the things my feet had seen in Rome. The doorbell rang; I got up to get my breakfast. I took the tray from the waiter, gave him a tip, and got back to the view I was enjoying on my private balcony at Hotel Del Senato overlooking the Pantheon. It was my favorite building in Rome; a city packed with magnificent monuments. I knew I must say good-by from this spot.

I couldn't possibly count the number of afternoons spent below this balcony at Piazza della Rotunda. In the summer I drank white wine and in winter I drank cafe macchiato with Colette and Godot at my feet. It was our last day in Rome and I watched how patiently my dogs sat waiting for our next address. I didn't think I was ready to be patient, I hadn't yet learned my lesson. But we had a couple of hours to kill before our flight so I put my feet up and enjoyed the building. It was pointless to worry about whether or not the moving van would arrive in Paris on time. Personal items were inconsequential compared to the history of the Pantheon.

Drinking my cappuccino and eating my two cornetti, I

couldn't help think how mild they tasted, how mild every-thing was except for the heavy emotional environs. I wanted to feel busy. I needed distractions. I imbibed my last gasp of calm and feasted my eyes on the facade recalling treasures inside; the tombs of Italian kings, a bust of Raphael with its elegant dome, its oculus providing the only source of natural light throughout the immense temple.

The only thing I knew was that it would take years to wrap my head around what it meant to live in the Eternal City. I was searching for a home but it wasn't Rome. The day before I'd given the long, ancient looking skeletal keys back to our landlord. I hoped it would relinquish the low-level stress I always had of losing them, or maybe it was the stress of trying to converse with some nuance, in someone else's language.

Maybe I loved Rome too much and thought my deep love went unrequited. I wanted something she couldn't give me because I didn't even know what it was, but that building remained the prettiest I had ever seen. Time no longer stood still, Paris was waiting, and far less patiently.

# 18

# PARIS: TIME FOR DELIRIOUS DISTRACTIONS

### 2006-2009

~

I expected Paris would demand affection and exceed expectations; in the same way I considered her a finite proposition. The dream was never to settle down permanently in la Ville Lumiere. My grand europhile fantasy was to move to Berlin after Paris and live in each for three years, completing a nine year trilogy experiencing 'Old Europe'. What I couldn't possibly know was how dramatically our lives would change at the end of our three-year lease; my mother would die, our financial situation would take a dramatic turn, and our marriage would suffer immensely under the weight.

When Muv died, friends tried to be helpful by saying things like, "You must embrace the grief." But I felt it was the other way around. Grief took me so tightly in its grip I couldn't let go. Eventually I had to take a trip to Auschwitz. It wasn't the most logical choice yet I had to go to Poland if only to remember how lucky I was to have blood running through my veins. To get back to the living and be grateful once again.

But what a way to go. If I was meant to lose everything, Paris provided an idyllic playground for my own *fin de siecle*. France proved to be the right country at the right time because the French responded to sadness directly, almost celebrating it and if it insisted on sticking around, *alors,* all the better. There's a reason for my favorite joke: "What do you call an Italian in a bad mood? French."

The cultures had so much in common. I watched mothers fawn over their sons far more than their daughters, but thought this produced bitchier results in French men. I wished I could have made more friends with Parisian women because they offered more sympathetic company. Moving from Rome to Paris felt absolutely natural. They spoke one another's language with ease and multiple topics overlapped, especially attitudes towards food. The French stick to their recipes while the Italians incorporate mother or grandmother's touch—both offering the freshest and finest ingredients, daily, for cooking from first principal.

Fashion reigns supreme and there were as many chatty egoists here as there. The few differences were dramatic because the French continue to live at the center of the universe whereas Italians happily rest on their laurels. The French remained obstinately convinced their elected officials must act on the citizen's behalf; hence the perpetual state of protest. French language dictated diplomatic precision whereas Italians boast at least a dozen ways of saying the same thing.

All it took was one swift flight aboard Air France, the most dog friendly of all airlines, to swap one capital for the other. Godot sat contentedly on my lap while Colette did pirouettes along the aisle entertaining our fellow passengers. Paris was going to teach me how to take fun seriously.

~

*...a hedonist*

~

IT DIDN'T HURT I managed to find a flat to satisfy all my hedonistic tendencies. Our new home was on a street with the longest name in Paris; Rue de la Montaigne Sainte Genevieve, located in the fifth arrondissement three blocks away from the Sorbonne. A neighborhood packed with students and eccentrics, replete with streets romantically named after poets and saints.

Outside our front door was one of the best markets in the city, Marche Maubert, located on Boulevard Saint-Germain. Beyond its convenience, the flat felt as funky as it was elegant: open and spacious with floor to ceiling windows spreading the entire length of the main salon. It had the prettiest views I'd ever seen. Directly in front of us the Eiffel Tower's blue lights sparkled brightly in the distance at sunset and immediately to the right sat Notre Dame. The slightest glance to the left caught the Pantheon looking down at us majestically and our entire flat was completely wrapped in Haussmann architecture. It was like a gothic and baroque fairytale, and it felt so close it became an extension of our living space.

Our bedroom was located at the back of the flat with windows along the walls and above our bed. Sometimes a quick, heavy downpour woke me up and by the time I walked around to the front our entire space was immersed in deep purple thanks to a rainbow perched across Our Lady of Paris. It was surreal without a straight angle to be found. In the middle of our U-shaped flat sat the tiniest kitchen I'd ever seen but after living on a boat I didn't mind. It felt familiar and it was easy to cook a four-course dinner for several guests. My sense of space had been eternally altered and Paris only served to enhance the effect.

When friends came to visit they might meander down the corridor to use our bathroom at the back, invariably I'd hear them say something like, "Bailey, have you seen this?"

I knew they'd caught some action from the bedroom right below. A famous soft porn actress from the 80's occupied this flat; now older, often self-medicated, tipsy or just noisy. She kept nothing confidential about her lifestyle, extending her personae off the stage and into a fun-filled afternoon in her bedroom with friends. She didn't inspire voyeuristic tendencies because we never got along. I'm not sure she got along with anyone after the way she took back her home. Initially, when we moved in, there was a nice Belgian couple living there, until she started camping at their front door for a week; they got the message and moved out. She was a piece of work. When taking Colette and Godot for an early morning walk I might see her coming home from a long evening, weaving along Boulevard Saint-Germain, her gaze unfocused, letting me escape from her view.

There was another pair of expats on the third floor. They were Vietnamese and the husband was the kind of artist who could make you feel calm just by walking into his apartment. His paintings sat far apart on a few walls, sparsely drawn, tranquil landscapes of his home country. I went to his art shows, and that couple balanced out the antics of the actress. To keep my affairs in order I got lucky and found a woman named Maryse. She worked for a couple of brothers on the second floor and helped keep my place clean once a week and proved critical with bills and paperwork I couldn't understand.

Maryse knew all the gossip in the building. One morning she took Colette and Godot for a walk. When the actress saw her she started yelling "Les American, Les American." Maryse found this profoundly funny and the actress gave the building a slightly decadent flair. The French love their artists and forgive them everything. I found this fair and just tried to stay out of the woman's way.

From the moment I saw that flat I wanted it so much we were willing to complete a lengthy and invasive dossier including six years of financials and work history. Not to mention a year's rent transferred to a French bank. The banker treated this large amount like a loan. This lets us in a little secret about why Europe looks to Germany for financial expertise.

When I picked up our keys at the real estate agent's office I noticed our 'dossier' sitting precariously close to the trash can at the end of an elaborate desk. When I asked about it the agent laughed and threw it into the drawer then gave me the most elegant keys I'd ever seen. A tubular shaped object, gilded with so many layers of serrated edges my keys looked more suitable for a Swiss bank deposit box than our front door. When I took them home I checked out our 'cave' located in the basement below with all the rat traps, and decided to stock a few cases of French wine alongside our suitcases and spare boxes, and then took the elevator to the top floor and let my new keys do their magic.

Once inside I was greeted by a wide, circular staircase with polished wooden steps guiding me up to the most stunning views. The flying carpet looked like it was made

for the place. It took me just three days to unpack everything and hang all our pictures. I couldn't wait to show it off.
I just needed to get out there and meet some people.

These keys reflected my approach towards navigating
my new city. It was a large labyrinth so I worked close from
home initially, extending our tour outward. I took Colette
and Godot for long walks and roamed the various neighborhoods, a complicated maze of arrondissements; four hours
flew by in a minute.

Papillons are accustomed to attention. Italian women
used to coo at Colette and Godot, with colorful variations of
"piccolo" and "canini"; and they would linger until I walked
away. A Frenchman offered only the most economic nod, his
appreciation was brisk, "c'est papillon" or "c'est petite
Chien" as he quickly walked by.

The thrill of driving my moto was over. Due to the
dossier experience, I dreaded another registration process
and left my motorcycle with friends in Rome. My timing was
good because cheap bicycle rental schemes were emerging
all over Europe. This encouraged me to promote my mode
of travel around town from foot to a silver bike with a
basket. Whenever I saw a petite girl fall off her vespa and
pedestrians running around, helping locate her high heels
in the middle of traffic, I missed my moto a little bit less.
Colette and Godot jumped up and down in excitement until
I lifted their little bodies into the basket, secure in their
blanket; where they fit perfectly.

A solo trip to Cafe de Flore took less than ten minutes
on foot where I sipped wine and *la soupe aux pois* with my
fellow posers. If I craved a longer sojourn on foot I might
find myself at Roland Garros. Anything felt possible in Paris.
This tournament, like Wimbledon, occupied such a large
portion of my youth, seen each year on television. At the

event I realized there was no need to procure tickets for center court. The glamour lived along the fringe, where I could do my research and wrap myself in nostalgia. The young Eastern European women captivated me. I contrasted them with my youth, thinking back to when I used to play cards with Tracy Austin at the Jack Kramer Tennis Club in Palace Verdes.

When summer hit the streets, protocol took an exit. Paris was no longer tidy. Instead, she became informal and messy. Especially on June 21st, the longest day of the year, when summer solstice inspired musicians and singers and electric guitars to occupy every single corner of the inner city from late afternoon to well past midnight. The noise was deafening so sleep was out of the question and you just had to get into the swing of things. Along the Seine they spread their blankets underneath their picnic baskets as people congregated everywhere and everyone danced with strangers along the river, beneath the boundless blue sky.

By the time autumn came around I found a new rhythm. I'd forgotten how much fun it was to be busy. Going to the ballet regularly at the prettiest opera house at Palais Garnier, or a taking a short trip across the river to the 4th arrondissement, to the Marais, for Opera at the Bastille. But the Comedie Francaise was both special and educational. I kept attending the same Moliere plays hoping it might improve my basic French. It never really did, yet long before curtain time, I positioned myself outside at Place de Colette eating Salade Nicoise like a typical tourist hoping to catch a glimpse of the handsome actors that hung out there before work. Paris made everyone feel sexy.

The expat community was large and easy to meet at English bookstores. My fellow Americans spun around the city in feisty and frenetic circles, desperate for invitations and introductions; they were a very different breed from those I met in Rome. Parisian energy invited a uniquely competitive type of behavior which could make me feel uncomfortable or maybe it was just one or two expats I found unsettling; I let them know I wasn't staying long but it could be a combative group.

The one exception was an American named Jim Haynes who had been hosting Sunday dinners since the 60's at his apartment in Montparnasse. The food wasn't great but that didn't stop him from charging twenty euro per person. Once I brought a friend visiting from San Francisco and he said, "What a scam." But it was worth it to socialize with my own tribe. I didn't miss home but I did miss my accent. I was also surprised by how many expats tried to monetize their apartments, though none did it with as much success as Jim. He gave off a rare and gentle quality letting his guests take over the apartment.

I created my own network of acquaintances and hosted dinner parties. I didn't share the same desire for invitations but the rewards followed my effort. There was no reason to turn down tickets to a couple of couture shows and art openings. The distractions demanded exploitation and one of the major benefits of living in the city of lights was the sheer diversity of humanity swimming throughout.

# 19

# JIM THE PRIEST AND MONSIEUR D

~

One week in particular illustrated this idea perfectly. On Monday I hosted a lunch for an Irish American priest traveling far away from his black parish in Chicago. Collarless and compassionate, Jim had just finished a year-long sabbatical at the Vatican. I was grateful to spend an afternoon together because I was still in reactionary mode against the evangelicals gaining political and cultural power in the States. This lunch stretched out for hours and the conversation was fun and feisty. We both felt right at home.

I listened as he volleyed back and forth between the brutal politics behind the Archdiocese in Chicago. He shared the texture of his life as a white pastor in a black parish. His recent sabbatical made the kind of impact that will last a lifetime. The politics were so subtle yet more potent than anywhere else. It was an intense discussion, and I could say whatever I wanted.

The following Thursday I was invited to live another kind of life at the home of Monsieur D.; to peek inside the life of a nineteenth century Frenchman. Monsieur D. was older, terrifically elegant and reserved. He had to be the son of an industrialist. My outfit was chosen with care. My closet had filled up with Issey Miyake thanks to the annual sale at the flagship store located at Place des Vosges. This was a key Parisian event because Miyake's creations became affordable if only for a few short hours. The French enjoyed a keen relationship with all things Japanese, and Parisians descend on the piles of accordion like material with gusto, giving me less than twenty precious minutes to successfully locate my own treasures each year.

However, Issey Miyake didn't suit this invitation; staying classic was critical. Buried in the back of my closet sat a pink and navy Chanel knock off. Muv had bought it at a non-profit event in Seattle and probably knew I might need it in Paris. My friend greeted me with approval and we made our way to Monsieur D.'s penthouse nestled in the Bois de Boulogne, a wealthy and leafy suburb of Neuilly.

His building boasted the most fantastic example of Art Deco I'd ever seen. I'd been inside a penthouse in Manhattan, full of originals lining the walls, but this was an elevated sort of affair. In the past I'd been served by a maid in Rome but Monsieur D.'s maid was a woman without age, as if born to wear that black and white uniform. The white cotton headpiece was glued to her dark hair, perfectly smooth, nothing out of place; the entire room felt dutiful, crisp, and completely contained. She came out of nowhere with great frequency, always on cue, enhancing the formality. At one point, I stole a glance beneath the ornate table, full of glass and gilded edges. I caught my host pressing down on an elevated portion of the creamy carpet with his beige suede leather shoe; so *that* was the secret behind the maid's perfect timing.

The luncheon stood in stark contrast to the one with the American pastor. Here, Monsieur D. dictated the behavior, followed by a long pause before starting the same subject over and over again; the aesthetics of art. I doubt he'd ever worked a day in his life. His time was devoted to architecture and fine art. The attitude and ambiance was subdued like the slate blue fabric lining the walls. He showed me a comprehensive collection of Jade from Asia and sculptures and installations from Egypt. Every item over 2000 years old.

We moved to the library for an aperitif and my host asked, "Would you prefer Handel or Mozart?" When my cafe macchiato was finished, he asked, "Would you like to take a stroll in the garden?" We took a little waltz around the top of the building; every scene on a Paris postcard on full display.

Then I was led back downstairs to the main salon and show; the art on his walls. And more walls, many pieces hanging without something as tedious as a frame. My host had the eye of an artist and the mind of a collector and quickly I realized why Monsieur D. was aggressively courted by both the Louvre and Musee D'Orsay. I was transported to another world but not without modern gadgets. Each time he pushed a button, another wall slid away without a sound, revealing more treasures beneath. When my host decided I had enough, which I had not, the art disappeared; my view was full of the Bois de Boulogne.

In one week my social life was filled by James the Priest; authentic, intent on enriching the soul in the only way he knew how. The next, by Monsieur D.; dignified, an effete aesthete who lived to enhance sensual pleasure through social etiquette and exquisite art. If one man leaned towards the spiritual, the other towards the materialistic, both missions were fulfilled adroitly.

*...heading towards the exit*

MY DINNER PARTIES lasted as long as my luncheons which often extended beyond the Roman experience. I was a hedonist. I wanted the wine to be fine and the food to be fantastic. However, the guests didn't provide the central entertainment. My favorite time were the hours before they arrived and after they left. Creating a beautiful experience mattered above all. Prior to my guests arriving the mornings were spent downstairs at Marche Maubert. I'd take my long shopping bag on wheels and walk across the street. When it was full it was time to go home. The stores were all conveniently lined up, first the wine shop, then the butcher, the bread and dessert store, before the grand finale, choosing the flowers and letting the colors spill out over the top of shopping bag. I'd discuss my menu at the wine store and keep the heavy bottles at the bottom. Then the vegetable stalls where ingredients were gathered for my eggplant bundles and salad. The butcher was always surrounded by fowl hanging above his head or turning around in his rotisserie, dripping fat on top of those highly prized potatoes. The bread shop was next door but I only bought dessert, preferring to serve grissini in goblets at either end of the table. The dessert was always a gelato or sorbet with some fruit and I saved the best for last; satiating my fetish for flowers.

I'd unpack the groceries and take out a favorite hand painted tablecloth. It was painted by a well-known local artist in Seattle named Robin deVick. After meeting Muv years before, Robin said, "I just want to be able to talk like her." Muv had a passion for birds and she inspired Robin to paint the happiest tablecloth I'd ever seen, splashed in birds in primary colors hanging off branches and leaves of cheerful green. After the flowers and candles and goblets found their places, the guests would arrive and once they left I could relive the event all over again.

My guests were expats, locals or friends stopping in from the States or somewhere else. Their stories were always the same yet I began hearing them with a different ear. I was spending less time traveling home. Every six months I went back and spent ten days running around seeing friends and spending less time trying to find another client. Perceptions once held dear were slipping away. If an American friend was trying to convince a French acquaintance why America was so special, I could now understand how it might fall on deaf ears.

Watching the news in another language was starting to penetrate my psyche. To many, like me, Gore Vidal came across as America's biographer but now his ideas of empire were beginning to take shape and make themselves known to the chattering class. We just didn't look or act like the good guys as much as we convinced ourselves we were. In the hours after my guests left I could focus on their stories and personalities and individual fears. I wasn't sure where I fit in but I knew I didn't want to move back to Seattle. That could only feel like moving backwards; another transatlantic trip was out of the question but Berlin didn't feel imminent. Our three-year lease was up in a couple of months but I couldn't imagine staying here. It was a silly life and I was starting to wonder whether or not Francis would ever come back to France.

# 20

## LA FIN

∾

I flew down to Malta every other month and it was always a hassle. Francis had rented a large villa but it came with consultants or the odd investor stopping in to hear the latest elevator pitch. It did not lend to intimacy. I couldn't even leave the airport without an argument. The Maltese officials never agreed or could believe dogs could enter their island. They loved the benefits of being a new member of the European Union but weren't updated on all its rules. Obviously they had never been to Switzerland. No one accommodates a dog like the Swiss. Colette had lived on more continents than I had, and my papillons traveled with me to over a dozen countries, including England and Scotland; I was well aware of island requirements. It didn't matter, the Maltese officials always made me sit in a little room while they argued, until I started arguing with them, and it was always a major hassle.

Malta felt isolating and was too small. It was packed with 400,000 residents that lent to noise pollution. And

Francis was perpetually stressed out. His IT company had a Follow The Sun Support Model, which proved a hard sell in the current market. They had offices in New Zealand and Seattle, and their main headquarters sat in Malta but clients weren't lining up. Francis was constantly trying to raise venture capital and I knew our own money was being spent but Francis was obstinate; he kept doubling down. Francis was so effective at putting a company together and making sure the infrastructure was a smooth operation, but sales were not part of his wheelhouse.

When I wasn't in Malta the long distant phone calls became increasingly tense. Francis didn't like the phone and preferred email. But I always called, "When are you coming home?"

Francis, exasperated, "Things aren't going well, I need to stay here, maybe next month."

The following month I called to ask, "When are you coming home?"

He was more honest, "It's too expensive to fly back and forth. I need to stay here. I have to make this work."

Then my father called. Muv was in the hospital. It was alarming because I talked with her constantly, often twice a week. I knew her routine. The Seattle Art Museum received a visit each week, she had lunch with friends. My father had disengaged and discouraged social activity, not Muv, she loved living downtown and its benefits. I kept abreast of her health and doctor appointments because of the incident five years ago when her blood cell count became an issue for the first time.

I called her at the hospital and asked, "Do you want to me to come home?"

Muv said, "I'm fine, darling, it's such a long way."

"Mother, it sounds like I need to be there. What are they telling you?"

She replied, "Not much, really, they're just trying to get my blood cell count under control. But I'll be fine, the doctors know what to do, I trust them."

She didn't sound right so I called her doctor for more information. Then I called Dr. Bob, we discussed the blood tests, and her previous incident. He said, "If I were you I'd get on the next plane."

I followed his advice and called Muv. I didn't share my conversation with Dr. Bob but I kept her on the phone for as long as I could. She didn't argue and I knew she was relieved.

I sat down in my favorite chair and avoided the views. It was a dismal day in early January. I scoured the apartment trying to avoid the fear that was seeping into my body until my eyes locked on a drawing she had sent out on her last birthday; August 16th. She had turned seventy-six and sent the card to me and two close friends in Northern California who happened to share the same date of birth. I had it framed and it sat on my library. For Muv, art provided creativity, and like many artists, it was a way to solve problems.

Her final sketch was drawn in black ink on an oblong white piece of paper. It could have appeared in a high-end fashion magazine because the subject was stylish and the dress elaborate. It was a self-portrait yet the woman was of an indiscriminate age, and she was walking away from the viewer dressed like a Russian princess. The hair was short, cupped under and landed on top of a high collar which fanned out dramatically, anchoring the dark hair perfectly. She had a small waist emphasized by a full skirt that stopped just below the knees. She was wearing short boots, but only one could be seen, as if the other was stepping into the abyss. Or was it heaven. The strokes were all done in crisscross fashion but the texture was so rich you could practically feel the fur at the top of the boots and the rich fabric, like embroidered tapestry. The significance of the drawing was lost on me when she sent it; now, the message as concise, as each line drawn in her last sketch.

The dense, short strokes filled out the ensemble and made it feel complete but the underlying message was a woman ready to hollow out her life, wishing to keep it basic while dressed well. The picture was full of movement with a fixed destination but the viewer couldn't miss the expressive state of grace. Her hands gathered up the heavy folds of fabric at either side, with ease, as if she was truly looking forward to stepping into the next dimension. There were a few lines drawn above, representing light clouds, with a soft mound of earth down below, to navigate; color would have detracted from the mystery.

Muv had written, in an arc, over the top of the woman, "The Spirit of '76". It was a breezy way of capturing her age and love of country, but her intuition and high state of consciousness were illustrated below the woman's feet. She had written, "Full Speed Ahead! Love, Alex". In her mind, the problem was resolved; she was simply going on another adventure.

Then her signature, below the elaborate skirt, "Alex".

I couldn't believe overlooking such an obvious clue. The sketch had affected me and it pleased others with its fantasy, but the dark reality now shook me deeply. In that second I knew my mother was going to die in the same way I knew I was sitting in my favorite chair. Our connection was so deep words only got in the way of emotion. That drawing made me dwell on the meaning behind her voice during our last conversation; she sounded tired, almost resigned.

I was alarmed. I needed to arrive in time. I needed to see her face and her body. I needed to be with her. I wanted to escape my apartment but fear kept me strapped into that chair. Fear and a future of not being able to hear that voice. Her style was admirable, as was her compassion, but her most significant trait was the sound that came out of her mouth. It never wavered or stuttered, it never sounded confused unless it was intentionally altered to make a point. Most of all it was filled with calm.

I looked around in desperation and found one of Muv's portrait's hanging above the dining room table. She had painted my oldest brother's daughter and captured her sweet essence at a young age. I tried to remember how she talked about that painting because it was unusual in its size, the heavy acrylic she used, along with the elaborate gold frame chosen. Muv had probably wanted her eldest son to have it but there was a touch of competition with our family's other artist. If my mother was self-contained, and she was, her art spilled over with quiet emotion.

I studied it keenly for the first time. My niece's light blonde hair was swept back from her face with a white bow at the back of her head. Muv's favorite artist was Mary Cassatt and the frock worn could have lived in one of her paintings. Even her feet were displayed in the same way, one foot turned slightly inward, like one of Cassatt's famous mother-daughter paintings. Muv painted her grand-daughter wearing an elegant long black dress, with small suede shoes and laces below, and up above the girl wore a soft smile with two tiny pearl buttons dropping down at the collar. Some white fabric peaked through at each wrist right above the young girl's hands.

The only thing I could remember was her comment about them, "Hands are the most difficult part to get right, they seem to take forever as if they hold the secret." My eyes focused on them as they lay lightly clasped on her lap, relaxed and perfect. When my friend Clair saw the portrait, she wanted Muv to paint her son. Muv hesitated because she preferred to choose her own subject but said, "Why don't you give me a polaroid and I'll think about it."

That photo lived at the corner of her easel for weeks. Then one day she surprised me with the portrait. Claire's seven-year-old son was painted in acrylic. He was young but Muv had captured his unusually defined features, and, she had captured his essence. Claire and her husband insisted on throwing her a dinner party. Whenever Muv asked for a photo of myself I always declined. She wanted me to go to a professional for a sitting. I never did. If I have one regret, that might be it.

Everyone thought we were so similar but we were not. Muv was cautious while I dove into projects with abandon; she moved in slow motion while my foot never found the brake pedal. She painted slowly but her favorite medium was watercolor because it forced her to pick up the pace. Yet on the very rare occasion when the sewing machine came out I thought her project might take forever.

She placed the sewing machine at one end of the dining room table and put the Vogue pattern at the other without opening it. She'd take a step back and think about the project, perhaps smoking a cigarette. Then she'd open the packages and lay out the tissues one by one, unfolding each piece carefully, respecting the thin paper. The pattern was age appropriate but the fabric could have been worn by an adult even though she was making dresses for two daughters under the age of ten. Finally she would move everything from the dining room table and spread it across the living room floor. She'd get on her knees and move methodically around the Persian rug, taking the pins from her mouth, attaching the fabric to the pattern. I would stoop down and hand them to her hoping it might speed up the process, but she barely took notice. She was utterly immersed in her project and there wasn't an ounce of tension in the room. If I was impatient, and I was, Muv acted as though she had all the time in the world. I kept staring at my flying carpet until it was time to pack.

Two days later I was in Seattle and rushed from the airport to her hospital room. Her head sprang up from the pillow when she saw my face, we both gushed, "Oh!" at the same time. I stopped inches away from her face. I noticed it was the first time she hadn't bothered to put on any make-up. She gently grabbed the collar of my Issey Miyake shawl and said quietly, "You're so beautiful."

The relief came and went too quickly as my eyes scanned the rest of her body. I tried to lay my hand on her upper leg but she was in pain. She tried to move her leg and said, "It's so awful, I just can't find a comfortable position."

From that moment on I shifted into autopilot. Instinctively I knew what to do. I don't think her doctor appreciated my presence but the nurses all seemed to like her, and I wasn't going anywhere. The second in command was a female doctor with short dark spiked hair. After a few days she said to me, "I want you around when I die."

At night I stayed with my father in their apartment. His dementia was getting worse and I knew he was grateful to have me there. A week flew by and I took her blood cell count numbers to Dr. Bob.

"She only has a few days left to live, Bailey."

I talked with the doctors and then I went into Muv's

room with the female doctor. We stared at one another and I said, "It's time for the morphine Mother, it will help your pain." She understood the implications and accepted my statement with the smallest nod.

When the female doctor left the room, Muv looked up at me and said, "I think she has a crush on you." Muv's humor was intact, her mental state remained unchanged, she was aware of everything around her but she wouldn't press the morphine button. She wanted to feel everything until the end.

Then we had another visitor and this one had a mission. She was carrying a bible. She looked down at Muv as if she was here to do her a favor, "I'm here to pray with you."

I was leaning against the ledge along the window and when Muv turned her head my way her expression told me everything I needed to know. She was utterly perplexed, as if this was the weirdest idea she'd ever heard. If my mother was private, the most private relationship she shared was with her God.

I wanted to laugh because it felt farcical having this stranger in the room suggesting we pray together. I moved towards her bed and said, "Really, we're fine." The woman wouldn't move. I said again, "Really, I mean it, but thank you." Muv stopped trying to find a comfortable position and placed her arms to either side and closed her eyes. The woman looked at me, then at Muv and knew her mission had failed; Muv had her own private line.

After a lifetime of talking there wasn't anything to say. Sometimes I would suggest she press the button but she responded by shaking her head. Then Sally came into the room for the first time since I arrived. She was wearing one of Muv's designer jackets. She stood there posing underneath the television set demanding attention. I moved back to the window and we stood in a triangle but only two lines connected.

"It looks just fine." The half-smile on Muv's face spoke volumes. She was in excruciating pain. It was a pitiful moment. Sally had spent a lifetime blaming our mother for everything, even her marriage. When I asked Sally about her divorce, she thought her response was awfully clever, "Well, I thought I married Dad, then I realized I married Mom."

I stood there and tried to decipher the mother-daughter relationship and two items came to mind; I realized Muv thought it was her job to mitigate the damage Sally did and more importantly, it no longer mattered. Muv didn't have the energy to deal with Sally's issues and her personality faded away. My eyes tried to focus on her frame and her latest obsession for body building. The jacket's lines looked bulky and she became vague. I gave her a blank stare as if she wasn't there. Muv looked to the ceiling and kept blinking her eyes. Sally looked down at her feet and walked out the door.

The following day I said, "Mother, can I write about our secret?"

I was surprised how quickly she responded, "When I'm gone you can write about anything you want darling."

"When I'm finished I'll dedicate it to you."

She looked up at me hovering above her pillow and said, "That the best news I've had all day," and gave me a final, quiet smile.

I knew it wouldn't be long and that's when I did something wrong.

"Don't you want to call Dad and say good-bye?"

Her response surprised me as she shook her head.

"Are you sure?"

She didn't move. I called him and put the phone to her
ear. My siblings arrived a few hours later. Sally looked at
Muv and then left the room. Each brother took one of her
hands. The middle brother said something about her not
being able to watch the news, and then he burst into tears.

Muv looked from one son to the other yet I knew, due to
her pain, she wanted to be alone. Now I understood why she
didn't want me to make that phone call.

More importantly, she did not want to be moved from
that hospital bed. They had moved her from Swedish
Hospital before I arrived for no apparent reason, and now
they were going to move her again. This was her worst
nightmare. She wanted to die on her own terms but they
wouldn't let her.

A large woman arrived on the scene and announced
they must move her to a hospice. I suspected they needed
the bed. Muv looked at me, wanting to shake her head, then
she looked back at the social worker. She was a formidable
woman. She crossed her arms and waited for the information to sink it.

"Can I come with her in the ambulance?"

The woman shook her head.

"I'll follow you in the car. I'll be right behind you."

When we arrived the proper paperwork had not. I sat in
the front room and paced, waiting for the fax machine to
authorize the morphine and additional equipment. Then I
heard my mother scream, "Bailey!"

I ran to the room and she started gasping for breath.
Then her head fell down on the pillow, her eyes closed and
her breathing became hard and constant.

Suddenly there was another man in the room and he
simply said, "It won't be long now."

I was stunned. I had the small bag she had packed and

took out her favorite Edith Wharton novel and started reading to her beside the bed. I didn't know if she could hear me but I just kept reading to her for hours. I cried, I touched her, and then I read as she offered a lesson in death.

Finally at midnight I was so exhausted I looked over at the small couch and couldn't resist. I hadn't slept for days. I laid down and pulled the small blanket up to my face. The minute I felt myself fading I bolted upright. Her last breath felt like an explosion. I ran to her side and studied her face. She was no longer in that body. I ran out of the room and the orderly came in and confirmed what I already knew. I kept feeling her forehead until it was no longer warm. I didn't want to leave and yet couldn't wait because that room was full of death.

I signed the paperwork. Suddenly, they were organized. I found my mother's car and drove down from that neighborhood packed with hospitals, or 'Pill Hill' as we used to call it. I drove down the streets, once so familiar, feeling like a foreigner. I took a right onto First Avenue, now full of ghosts. It was January 17th and the city was pitch black.

It was past midnight as I turned around to close their apartment door and saw my father step outside their bedroom. "She's gone, Dad."

He looked down at the carpet and began shuffling in reverse, as if he could turn back time. He was back to sleep in minutes. I opened a bottle of red wine, full of self-pity, and cried until it was empty.

The following day was the kind of day you want to forget. Muv's doctor called and said, "I'm so sorry to hear about your mother. I'm genuinely shocked. I didn't think it would happen so quickly." I believed him. Muv never complained. For a while she shared a room with another patient who was vocal with her pain but Muv kept quiet. If there was a bill to pay at the end she was ready to settle it.

My father called my siblings and then he asked me to start calling everyone else. My eldest brother, the artist, wanted to talk to me. He said, "Thank you."

I found Muv's 'Birthday Book' by the phone and started dialing.

When I called Diana she said, "You will assimilate her, Bailey, you will."

When I called Phyllis she just said, "Oh." I couldn't believe it. That was not the aunt I remembered but it was the twin Muv had known all along.

I continued dialing and then my father said, "You need to call Victor."

I hesitated then dialed his number, expecting his wife. Victor answered and was shocked. After relaying the details there was a long pause. Then we started crying softly together until the flood gates burst open and words were no longer necessary; we only made sounds. An entire lifetime of emotion flowed from one end of the phone to the other for several minutes. If this was all I was going to get, I took it.

When I put the receiver down I was spent. My father was next to the window lost in the view. He said, "We need to call Carolyn later because he has short term Alzheimer's, he remembers everything, but not short term."

A few hours later Carolyn arrived home and called us back. My father made a gesture asking me to pass along the phone. He took the receiver, walked into his bedroom and closed the door. There was no need to put my ear to the door, I was no longer curious because it no longer mattered. Everyone had known all along and I felt nothing.

I walked over to my mother's love seat and noticed her knitting bag on the floor, tucked in between the leather settee and the table. There was something shiny inside. I picked up the embroidered bag and pulled out a tiny picture of Blaine. His head had been carefully cut out of a larger photo. I could practically see her meditating on that tiny memento. It was no larger than a passport photo but it must have meant the world to her.

When my father came out of the room he said, "Carolyn couldn't believe it. Victor was able to relay every single detail back to her when she came home."

My world had become one of confusion but this came as no surprise. My father was comfortable bringing up Victor, as long as he was initiating the conversation. He walked into the kitchen and poured himself a glass of water. I put the photo back into her bag and got up because I could see he looked deeply confused. His knees started to buckle and we cried on one another's shoulder for a few minutes. He was so frail and he had depended on my mother for everything.

She took care of the finances, the household, and I remember her saying once, "He is a Mama's boy, there is no doubt." I went through her closet and found a picture of Muv on a double date, she was a teenager but didn't look it. She and her girlfriend were in cocktail dresses laced with organza fabric, a feminine touch from the 50's with pearls worn around the necks. I was taken aback by how large Muv's smile looked when she was young, everyone was smiling, except her date. The couple to her right both had blonde hair and bright eyes. Muv looked dark and dramatic with her deep brown eyes but it was her date that got my attention. He looked like a doppelgänger for Victor Mature, so dark and swarthy and silent and strong. This was one of the few photos kept in her personal box for almost six decades.

My father was fair with bright blue eyes. When he was

young he was almost beautiful, tall, athletic but sinewy with a soft presence. Looking at that ancient photo made Victor appear inevitable.

Diana had said, almost emphatically, "Take everything you want, Bailey."

I packed some of her clothes, in particular her sweaters; knowing they would keep me warm. And I also took that photo of the four young people on their double date.

My parents had named me executor of their estate which meant I would have to take care of their affairs from across the pond. I was happy to do it but on that day, in their small apartment, our mutual depression became claustrophobic. My mother's touch was everywhere and yet she was nowhere to be found. I suggested we take a walk along the waterfront and have some coffee at the market.

We walked in silence until I said, "You know she called me a couple of months ago and was really fed up with the family drama, it was the first time she relayed her frustration like that. I thought it had ended with Blair's death, but why do you think there was so much resentment?"

His reply was too swift, "Because you always knew how to get what you wanted in life, Bailey."

It sounded right until I realized he was talking about himself. He had never taken any risks. When he retired early I asked him why and he said, "Because it made me feel better."

I felt sorry for him and his loss, but most of all I felt confused. I spent a few more days organizing my father's life knowing the siblings would start spending time at the condo if only to take control. It was too easy to forecast their actions and I just wanted to leave Seattle. The following Sunday I went to our church in Magnolia and a few of Muv's closest friends huddled around me in the back pew before the service. It was comforting to feel loved and to know how much they had loved her.

I listened to the sermon but was surprised how often Jesus was mentioned. I only remembered God, but then it may have been my own ears hearing what I didn't want to hear. So much had changed in such a short time, and the hardest times were yet to come.

Muv's death overlapped with an important event in Seattle. The judge who married us in the court house was going to be elected Superior Court Judge. Judge Richard Jones was an exceptional man and I had taken him to lunch or stopped by to say hello whenever I was in Seattle. One time he told me, "My brother once said the passport was the most important book in life." His brother also happened to be Quincy Jones and he shared some fun stories about him after I wrote him a long letter about Blaine and what my brother had meant to me.

I was invited to the elaborate event but I was an emotional wreck. I shouldn't have gone but I was so happy for his success. A family friend from childhood was there; she and her husband were politically involved in Seattle and they were also friends from our church. The woman, Judy, had lost her beloved twelve-year-old daughter in a freak sledding accident one winter, long ago. At her daughter's funeral, when I came through the line, she grabbed me and talked about how much promise her daughter held. It was a devastating moment as if I had triggered something; her pain was palpable.

When she saw me at this event so many years later she took me aside once again and said, "Bailey, you must embrace the grief."

The loss of a child is not something you ever recover

from and I would recover from Muv's death, I might even assimilate her, as Diana said, but it would take time.

I had witnessed my own country's pathologies and now it was time to experience my own. Joan Didion wrote about the difference between an uncomplicated death and a complicated one. Muv had given me a lesson in death but I was about to enter a period of pathological grief. I loved her intensely and now I would miss her more; it would prove excruciatingly hard to let go. Thankfully, Muv remained the lesson that kept on giving.

# 21

# EMANCIPATORY TOUR TO AUSCHWITZ

2009

∼

I called our Parisian landlord to let him know the lease wouldn't be renewed. I stopped going to the ballet and the opera. There was no need for another dinner party. We made the decision to move to Malta and I didn't even care. We put our 'home' in storage. I couldn't imagine we would stay long.

In the meantime I took a tour of Eastern Europe. It was time to go to Auschwitz. I packed my suitcase and took Colette and Godot in their carrier from one train to the next. After Slovenia we stopped in Budapest. After dinner I went to the bar and met a Jewish couple. After a few drinks I said, "My mother died. I'm going to Auschwitz."

The wife was taken by surprise and the husband replied, "I get it."

We arrived in Poland and I left Colette and Godot in the hotel. I could practically hear Colette asking me, "Why are we here?"

I answered out loud, "I don't know, I just need to be."

I spent the following day roaming aimlessly without a guide. I went to the death block and the executioner's wall. There was an assortment of flowers from Irish students full of cryptic prayers. Someone suggested I write a letter to Muv. I wrote it on a Franz Kafka postcard and looked for a place to put it and thought, 'anywhere but here'.

I walked through the holding cells where victims 'lived' before being massacred. I thought about Primo Levi's book *If This Is a Man*, and tried to imagine where one of the Jewish visitors once hid. It must have been somewhere in the museum. Apparently he stayed overnight because he thought he could experience the terror of his ancestors.

I folded the postcard in my hand, making it smaller, thinking about the few that managed to escape. There was one by the name of Rudolf Vrba, originally from the town of Trnava, in Slovakia. I decided I would travel to his home town and bury the letter there.

I took a taxi to the 'residence of death' a larger and darker space. It was called Auschwitz II. My eyes remained fixed on the Gate of Hell, the archway beneath the tower with just enough space for a train to pass through. I walked to the top of the tower and surveyed the scene. I remembered the dark hour following Muv's death, when I had to dial for a crematorium to take her away.

I left the tower and walked up and down long, wide paths where people waited to work or die. I walked for two hours without a destination until I suddenly felt like a meth addict who had miraculously survived the blast. I could barely move. Mentally I began counting my fingers and moving my toes. I was still alive. It was time to stop dwelling on the dead. Muv's message had been, "Full speed ahead!" Hadn't I been listening?

I wanted to run down the rest of the desolate path and

reverse my journey through the gates of hell and scream, "I want to live, really I do!" But my feet were so heavy, all the activity was in my head. I could only stomp my feet on top of the earth, I wasn't ready to step into the abyss. Gratefully, I fell into a taxi and prayed the train was on time so I could leave Auschwitz and all that it implied.

I stayed overnight in Slovakia and buried the letter near the hotel, a place that felt surreal, for completely different reasons. When I woke up the following day and went downstairs for breakfast the hotel was full of tennis courts. The breakfast room had large windows overlooking energetic, young women pounding tennis balls across the row of nets with enthusiasm. They were mostly young girls, they looked so young and powerful, hitting that little round ball with determination and precision; completely focused on their future. I thought of the past, and Paris, and Rolland Garros, then I placed my focus back on the young women. It made me feel a little hopeful, for a moment.

# 22

## MALTA: WHEN TIME FELT LOST

~

F rancis had fallen head over heels in love with Malta but I couldn't even muster a crush. If my odyssey was a series of interviews with various countries, this was the shortest; from the moment our eyes met we both knew this relationship wasn't going to work.

It's not like Malta isn't a great land to try to understand, this tiny island situated between Libya and Sicily, often forgotten on most maps. For many, it was considered a holiday destination, and for European parents, the middle of the Med remained a safe place to send their kids to learn English. For English expats, it was their idea of a great getaway, where they could consume cheap alcohol under the hot sun. To me it felt comparable to Gibraltar; unfortunately I was neither a fan of Madi's previous home nor was I here on holiday.

We never discussed moving our things to Malta. We were broke so we put our stuff in storage, packed several suitcases, and just got on the plane with Colette and Godot.

Francis had bought plenty of furniture for his 'work' related villa, so a furnished flat wasn't necessary, the stuff was familiar enough. My mental state tainted the experience, but if Malta was small it was also loaded with 7,000 years of history. I carved out enough time to jump off another cultural cliff.

If I'd lived in Malta prior to Rome and Paris, perhaps I could have viewed it through another lens. I was guilty of falling in love with countries that spent their energy creating art worth viewing, wine worth drinking, food worth eating, and style the world wanted to wear. As far as I could figure, all of Malta's energy had been devoted to defending its small, albeit strategically located island, which dictated a defensive personality. If Italians appeared weighed down by their history, the Maltese were positively buoyed by it. Every single one of their 400,000 residents seemed extraordinarily proud of their country; you couldn't help but feel it because everyone was stuffed into such a small space. They were eternally defiant. What they lacked in height they made up in self-identity; I found this both irritating and infectious.

For an island this size, it generated an awful lot of noise. Each week the Maltese found something else to celebrate which meant another festival with fireworks. They didn't start shooting them off at night like other people; the party began at 7am. If I needed to forge my way into the future, the culture constantly pulled me into the past, compelling me to embrace my depression even more. When the residents got tired of their island, they went to Gozo, another island in the Maltese archipelago. Gozo was the second largest in the seven island chain with 31,000 residents. This is where people went to escape, which they did by taking their car on a ferry and camping for long weekends.

People came for the view and this was the last thing I

wanted to see. After sailing across a large portion of the Mediterranean, the island made me feel like I was still at sea, or rather lost at sea. I could practically hear the water gods laughing at me, "You risked your lives and gave up everything to end up here, Ha!" The sea emphasized the distance separating me from the continent of Europe. While we were aboard *Madi*, even in the middle of the Atlantic, we had a fixed destination. Here I felt rudderless and lonely. It felt like failure.

Visiting *Madi* at the marina did nothing to adjust my attitude. Every day she received a cruel beating by the sun. She suffered major damage and was bone dry. I doubted either of us would recover and the climes were brutally unkind to a teak boat. I relegated her brightwork to Francis but he never did any varnishing. The only attention *Madi* received was from his office windows overlooking the marina.

It was not only useless but counterproductive to complain to Francis. If I questioned his love for Malta it only served to create a wider gulf between us. There certainly was an awful lot of tension in our new holiday home. Our marriage was fragile. For the first time since our transatlantic crossing we were together without a break, each miserable in our own way. We took our marriage vows seriously, but our commitments diverged; Francis was devoted to a failing company and I was content to let my grief take as long as necessary.

I braced myself for the answer but had to ask, "You could settle down here, couldn't you?"

He answered so quickly as to be spiteful. "Absolutely."

I fantasized about leaving him, and Malta. I fantasized about taking a slow cruise ship back to the States with Colette and Godot. I wouldn't have to be on watch or record vital information by scribbling notes in a log book at midnight. I vocalized these fantasies but neither of us took them seriously because we couldn't afford to. I even thought of putting some stones in my pocket and taking a long walk into the water but it was the kind of idea that lasted less than ten minutes. Like everything else; I was miserable and would have divorced myself if I could.

Strangely enough, lurking deep in the recesses of my mind, I remained oddly confident Malta couldn't possibly be a long-term proposition. Or maybe I hijacked that specific quality from my host country and insisted on my own mental defiance. Either way, his company couldn't get off the ground. The investment trickled in instead of offering a large impact with too many Peter Pan personalities running around impeding progress. Francis treated it like a family. This did not portend well but it didn't stop Francis but experiencing his own major denial. To me he looked vulnerable out on this frontier. The business model was a hard sell. He was ahead of the curve in understanding the benefits of a company located in Malta, but he had bet on the wrong horse. His least attractive trait was his obstinacy and Malta brought out the worst. I just had to wait and persevere, and assist where I could as he'd bet our life savings on it. For better or worse; it was time to learn about the Maltese.

～

*...cultural realities*

～

POLITICALLY THE MALTESE split right down the middle. One half of the island was glued to one party and they switched at each election. They weren't polarized, instead they had solidarity in everything, including height and hairstyle. Maybe I met one woman with short hair. They advertised blondes in their tourist literature yet I never saw a natural one. I never could decide whether the Maltese reflected the East or West. They insisted they identified with Italy but it didn't present itself through their food or style. They had a strong relationship with Libya which was exploited by selling the Libyans boat loads of unnecessary stuff and securing building contracts that allowed them to market their version of European architecture.

The Maltese version of Catholicism was uniquely their own. Unlike Italians they wore it in such heavy fashion it felt manufactured. There was too much gratitude towards St. Paul. Apparently he was ship wrecked on their island after being caught in a violent storm en route to Rome. Archeologists confirmed this happened in A.D 60. The site of this supposed ship wreck was marked with a grand statue in a town called Valetta which happens to be their capital. It should have been easier to believe; I too felt ship wrecked.

Malta shares no borders with any other country, and I concluded the people reflected neither the East or West; they were distinctly Maltese. Yet many of the residents were trilingual. They spoke their own language at home, derived from the Phoenicians, they learned Italian by watching Italy's RAI TV at night and practiced it when traveling to Sicily by ferry. They spoke English during the day in public places when necessary. This was impressive.

Malta carried a specifically patriarchal flavor which turned me off, but the pirate-like atmosphere appealed to men. Other than the sun loving, alcohol imbibing English, there were only a handful of Americans dispersed throughout the island. The men were far more enthusiastic than the women I met and neither provided a source of company. Francis had his own form of escape: he would take his motorcycle for a cruise across the island. Sometimes I came along for the ride because it didn't last longer than an hour or two.

I learned a little bit about Malta. I explored the Siculo-Norman period, I visited two or three Renaissance towns and Baroque villages on display. I learned about Malta's "Golden Age" when the Knights of St. John ruled the island, when the British introduced the neoclassical style seen at St. John's Cathedral. I heard a story about Berlusconi and how he came to Malta to negotiate his first media deal. I heard about how Kim Jong-il received his English language education at the University of Malta, and how he had been a guest of Don Mintoff, Malta's former Prime Minister. I heard how Mintoff told the CIA to take their money and go elsewhere. That was impressive as well. Not many leaders carry that kind of nerve.

What did turn me on was Malta's recent conversion to the Euro currency. In fact they were in charge of printing it. Europeans love nothing more than crossing borders, and the vast amount of monies lost had stopped when they formed the European Union. However, trade didn't trickle down smoothly to Malta, and shopping for groceries was a daily disappointment. They didn't use any pesticides, which was good, but this meant the meager selection of vegetables lasted no longer than a day. The fish was fantastic but I didn't want to eat fish every day.

By the time I was officially domiciled on the island in 2009 the women were starting to enter the work force in high numbers. They were beginning to fight for their rights and with confidence. Their frustration pierced through the air when I heard their constant refrain, "Oh my Got! Oh my Got!"

I spent time working with Francis but the need for my skillset proved inconsistent. I tried to help with sales in Seattle, through my contacts, but the deals were never closed. It was easy to get frustrated and easier to get bored. Sometimes I would take comfort in a few vodka tonics before dinner. I hadn't drunk hard alcohol since high school. It felt severe and like most ideas I had on the island, it eventually disappeared.

It wasn't as if I didn't try and find something to do but my meager attempts lacked follow through and became comical. The gaming industry was large on the island so I went out to investigate. I met with a Ukrainian lawyer along the way, and she shed light on the industry but the locals kept their network tight and secure.

Francis and I discussed marketing his IT services to Libya. I tried to get a visa and even studied up on the political 'Green Book' written by Gadaffi. After several trips to the embassy it proved impossible to obtain a visa and I never went to Libya. I was tasked to fly to London for an IT conference in hopes of helping his company market their services. I passed out cards and found an American marketing specialist whom Francis hired, but after a few months it wasn't a good fit and fizzled, in this we were consistent. Failure was felt on a weekly basis.

# 23

# THE SOCIAL SEASON

~

I started to socialize by getting an invite to an Embassy party. This proved as easy as inviting myself. I tried to be impressed with our American Ambassador but I can't remember his name. Then I went to a pig roast at a bar called "Dimples". The community was raising funds for a woman who suffered a motorcycle accident abroad and didn't have health insurance. I noticed four women sitting on a bench. Four women with short hair, like me, so I went to investigate. I tried to bond but stopped because I thought they might beat me up. The gay community was not out in the open in such a conservative environment and perhaps they were suspicious of my motives. I just wanted to have a chat.

I attended an event at the Monti Kristi Winery and listened to a new European Parliamentarian candidate develop and hone his message. Malta didn't feel like Europe so I might be forgiven for thinking the speech sounded more opportunistic than inspirational.

We visited the Inquisitor's Palace which happened to be the official residence of the Prime Minister of Malta. I met his wife, Katherine Gonzi, among the genteel gardens. She was kind and gracious, but the only true highlight of my social season unfolded during a business dinner with Francis. We met a young businessman who could have been David Cassidy's doppelgänger. I was giddy, young again, with a severe crush. This guy had no idea who David Cassidy was and I'm certain he thought I was mad but it was a perfect way to waste away a memorable evening in the middle of the Mediterranean.

Then I attended a business breakfast. It was called "How to take total advantage of the Obama Zillion-dollar Stimulus package." I tried to remain serious but it was funny. I listened to a German, one who happened to be living in New York, instruct a group of Maltese business men how to take advantage of my tax dollar. He offered advice on how to sell their innovative IP to businesses in the railroad or solar industry. Malta didn't have trains or solar but the breakfast was pretty good.

I worked on obtaining my Italian passport and came painfully close to success. Paying homage at the Italian Embassy was no easy feat. After another Herculean effort to get a document I had every right to own, the women at the Embassy decided they would not assist. I provided them with no less than fifteen documents. Apparently two were missing. That was the good news. The bad news being they wouldn't tell me which two were missing.

Malta was a dead end in every way. I missed Rome. I would always miss Rome. I often thought about Gore Vidal's response to being asked why he spent a third of his life living in the Eternal City, and he offered a reply lifted from

Howard Hughes, the notoriously wealthy and long-nailed recluse who once said, "I guess I just drifted into it." Yes. That man reflected my experience in Malta, like I was living in a sealed hotel room and going a little crazy.

I still loved to swim but when I read about the Portuguese Man of War jellyfish infecting their beaches I opted to swim laps at a local outdoor pool. After a few days I got my first eye infection. I went to the doctor and he called it 'dry eye' and gave me some medication which didn't seem to help. Malta was not a sympathetic place for me.

Like anywhere, individually the Maltese were nice enough, and there was a woman I quite liked. Actually they were two friends who happened to clean our flat, they came in each week but appeared to operate as one person. There was the dominant one, her name was Rose, and I never learned the other name because she only took orders and conversed directly with Rose. One week, while cleaning our place, Rose offered to take me to the races.

The Maltese version of horse racing was both humane and charming. The track was relatively soft and kept the weight off the horse's delicate bones. The riders directed the horses from behind, seated in a small cart, and absolutely no whips were allowed. The race began with a gentle gallop and gradually built up some speed and went around the track twice. It was dramatic and then it was over. The bets started at one euro and didn't move much from there.

∾

*...defeated, time to move on*

∾

THANKFULLY, our time in Malta was drawing to a close, and quite frankly I was surprised it lasted as many months as it had. Francis paid all the employees their severance pay for which they were grateful as well as providing valuable training in the IT industry. But the venture had failed. The company was gone, along with our savings, but apparently there was still hope. Francis spent another month meeting with people and investigating IT opportunities. I went along and tried to assist but it felt like a joke. When we met with a minister in the government he was far more interested with his real estate and Libyan schemes than discussing technology.

If there was one meeting to encapsulate everything, it was a meeting with a man who was 'connected', apparently he sat on several local 'Boards'. Somehow we got on the subject of Japan and swords, probably because he was selling cheap knock-offs online, along with T-shirts.

I said, "Francis has an original 'Katana' he bought in Japan, it's beautiful, you can feel the energy."

This guy sat across from us and kept implying it was a fake. Francis didn't feel the need to defend himself but everything I disliked about the island was represented in that short guy and his fake swords and cheap T-shirts.

I didn't say anything after that but thought of all the time Francis had spent in Japan when he worked for Microsoft. He truly loved the country and did research before buying this unique sword, appreciating its craftsmanship, not to mention the letter of authentication that came with such an investment. Sometimes I would take it out and complete the elaborate cleaning ceremony and I could feel the months of work and expertise that went into producing such a sword. If I didn't share his love for the country I shared his enthusiasm for the sword because it was, in a word; awesome.

I felt like we'd been suckered into Malta. Francis had devoted so much time and received so little in return. I couldn't help notice what the tourist office didn't want anyone to see. The dirt and the oil from cars were baked into the cement by the sun. In Rome we experienced the Scirocco winds that came in from the Sahara but they eventually washed away. Here in Malta, water was scarce, even though we were surrounded by it, but they couldn't wash down the streets. To drink the water from the tap meant taking your life in your hands. They still had rickety buses that were sixty years old. For some this was charming, for me it felt kind of dangerous.

I was able to locate two treasures on the island, and they were both painted by an Italian. Two of Caravaggio's masterpieces covered the large walls of the main Cathedral on Valetta. When visiting I felt close to the artist's dark heart because this is what Malta inspired in Caravaggio. It didn't help the artist was on the run after killing a man in a fight in Rome. The painting was called "The Beheading of St. John the Baptist". It was dark and dramatic and often I looked at that painting as if I too had lost my head.

Francis was finished with Malta but he would always admire the island, the people and his friends. There were undeniable benefits for business and tax purposes. A Maltese lawyer could write an entire contract on one page. The process required to domicile on the island was relatively painless. But the only hope we found arrived in the form of a contract in Geneva. Francis secured an IT project in Switzerland. We could move back to the continent. I was relieved. I was the boxer's daughter and I had persevered.

I embraced my last task which was to find *Madi* a new home. Fortuitously I found one located an hour from Venice, in a marina called Punto Faro in Lignano Sabbiadoro. It was full of Swiss, German, and Italian boats; they had one slip available and we took it, at last; success.

# 24

## SAILING TO LIGNANO SABBIADORO

~

W e had cruised to Sicily on *Madi* before so we opted to sail straight through to Crotone, a port city in Calabria. God was kind and we were back on the land where coffee tastes like a milkshake and pasta is al dente. We arrived at the heel of Italy, at Porto Vecchio, and parked next to the reddest boat I'd ever seen. Red sails, red interior, exterior, wheel, everything, owned by an older French couple. We chatted with our new, eccentric neighbors and I watched a vespa fly by on the dock. There must have been half of a family on that tiny moto and not one of them wearing a helmet. My body relaxed into the rhythm of southern Italy surrounded by style and laughter.

We docked at Santa Maria de Leuca in the province of Lecce. That night we went out for dinner and met a dynamic father and daughter duo from Genoa. Soon our table was full of sailors and solidarity. We happily gravitated towards one another, comparing notes, which was immensely useful as we were cruising in opposite directions. The father had just sailed along the Dalmatian Coast which happened to be our next destination. After eating fresh fish and drinking local white wine we drank Mirto on their 50 foot Beneteau into the late night. Black lights were strung along the dock giving a gorgeous touch of the locale. Life became better by the day.

Francis's IT project had a start date and we had a schedule to maintain. We had one glorious month to cruise the Dalmatian Coast and learn a little about Croatia. First we had to reach the eastern tip of Italy so we cruised up to the Adriatic until it connected with the Ionian Sea; where Italy sits directly across from Albania. Then we stayed in Otranto, a memorable port, and spent a week refueling, addressing issues, and preparing the documentation required for leaving the EU.

Otranto was atmospheric with its famous "Castello Aragonese". This castle inspired the first gothic novel in English literature called, "Otranto's Castle". At sunset the city center burst open with the most colorful street artists I'd ever seen. We anchored out for a couple of days, which was cheaper and more fun. At night we were serenaded by the coolest blend of techno opera music I'd ever heard.

Otranto also gave me a glimpse into how the Italian police operate. When I went to the town center for an errand I found myself in the middle of a drug bust. The method of rounding up petty criminals was a deeply subdued exercise. I didn't notice anything until I saw two policemen talking to a couple of drug dealers in front of a building next door. They coerced and handily manipulated the drug dealers and gradually got closer as one hour slipped into the next. This tribe has been talking for an awful long time. Everyone appeared so relaxed, even my fellow onlookers, without a hint of drama or violence hanging in the air. Ben Johnson would be immensely proud. The art of conversation was alive and well near the Ionian Sea.

Croatia came as advertised. It was pristine, untouched, and indisputably one of the most gorgeous coastlines in the world. In the past, when we cruised up to Canada we were surrounded by history, but this tour was accompanied by grand castles and cathedrals. Beyond the barely touched landscapes we were quietly exposed to recent wars with memorials and history lessons. The sea was becoming my friend again. There were borders, barely there, and there was an awful lot of solidarity; I was back in Europe.

It felt like I was getting prepped for Venice because Croatia is ripe with Venetian design. We walked underneath their version of "the bridge of sighs" with its tiny windows allowing the convicts one last gasp of their home town before death. Croatia reminded me of many things. It was deeply green like Seattle, and then it took me further back to Northern California with its bright sun and deep red stucco roofs overlooking palm trees and pungent pine. I forgot how sweet the smell of pine could be. Cypress trees and Baroque cathedrals and Renaissance palaces completed the picture. Dubrovnik provided drama with its gothic sensibility surrounded by fortified walls. It was a terrific town to stroll through and it could be done rather quickly. Then it was time to go back on the boat and float by Korkula island which happened to be Marco Polo's birthplace. Islands were scattered everywhere full of limpid bays, craggy bluffs, and vineyards. The coast line was unspoiled and drop dead gorgeous.

Our final port gave us one grand history lesson. We sat on two blue fold-out chairs aft deck and took in the three monuments before us. To our left stood the grand imperial opulence of the Austrian Habsburg culture, slightly to her right we saw the coliseum, as magnificent as the one in Rome. Then our eyes sat the flat and drab communist architecture inspired by Tito. All three laid out before us one afternoon as we sat at the back of *Madi*, amazed and grateful to take it all in.

We arrived in Lignano Sabbiadoro and found a tiny slice of heaven located in the province of Udine, in the Friuli-Venezia Giulia region of northeast Italy. Our marina was next to one of the main summer resorts on the Adriatic Sea. The town used to be called Lignano but they added Sabbiadoro to highlight the golden sand along her beaches. Beaches full of colorfully striped umbrellas lined up for miles. It felt like someone's fantasy of a sporty playground with golf carts delivering groceries and sundries to the boats securely moored by long sturdy posts, Venetian style. We prepared for Geneva, yet Lignano Sabbiadoro would insist I come back, if only to change my life.

# 25

# GENEVA: WHEN TIME FELT SERIOUS

~

Geneva was a such a wealthy city it made me feel poor. It wasn't the first time I didn't have any money, so the concept wasn't new, yet Geneva had a way of underlining it, then putting an exclamation point at the end. The environment felt dead serious, and very cold in the winter of 2009. It suggested, in a very stern voice; "It's time to get back on your feet, now." But I wasn't quite ready to get back on my feet. There was nothing romantic about our neighborhood except that a short train ride took us into the city center. Our apartment was tiny, slightly dingy, with a few furnished items to sit on and sleep in. There was no need to decorate but it's amazing what fresh linen and a vase of store bought flowers can do. The landlord was a small Portuguese woman with dyed blonde hair who knocked on our door to pick up the rent each month.

I grew up looking at Mount Rainier every day yet she kept her distance in Seattle. Here the alps were up close and

personal. They towered over us and they were truly magnificent. Every once in a while Francis would throw me over the
fender and drive his motorcycle up to Mont Blanc. In the
winter it was freezing, in the spring it was divine.

Geneva was utterly international and geared towards
expats who accounted for 40 percent of the city's residents.
Geneva also held about 40 percent of the world's wealth so
they were easy numbers to remember. Geneva was compact,
easy to navigate and I attended meetups at lovely restaurants with low lit lamps and expensive food and drink. If I
thought we had crossed some miles in our lifetime, I met
people who traveled far more than I could even imagine.
Everyone was constantly in the process of arriving home or
preparing to explore another part of the world. Francis had
family that worked at the UN and you tripped over them
every step of your way in this global city.

The muted grey and taupe architecture was easy to
admire and when you met someone for lunch, punctuality
was expected. It wasn't just their world famous watches; it
was the way stuff got done. The Swiss are serious and they
have their peculiarities. If you don't watch your garbage they
will watch it for you. If you wanted to become a citizen you
better know one of their three languages, with some fluency;
French, German, or Italian. And you better have an
astounding grip on their history, their referendums, and
why those cantons create the most democratic country of
them all. And you better be able to afford it.

They aren't a social tribe but in the cities they were stylish. Women wore mink coats and men stood at the train
stations wearing beautifully made hats full of feathers and
pins. I loved those hats and they were familiar, worn by
Germans in Bavaria and Italians in the north. Even I had
one. It's a place for UN workers and a place for bankers, it's a

state of mind for business and diplomacy. It felt like I was living within a postcard. Everything about Geneva was specific and efficient including the soft grey architecture set against the dramatic white and grey Alps.

I worked on my resume for the first time since arriving in Europe. I sent it out and waited. One morning I got a call from a German headhunter, a young man named Stefan, originally from Munich. I went on a series of interviews. They wanted me to convince them I could replicate my success in Seattle, and they wanted this done fast. I went on three separate interviews but couldn't seem to close the deal. I wasn't sure if it was my lack of confidence or the foreign environment. Or maybe I couldn't recreate what I'd done in Seattle. Everything was different; including me.

Moving from Malta to Geneva had a jarring effect and I felt off balance. Geneva was a place for people with immense focus and solid intent. In Malta I felt lost, in Geneva, I felt overwhelmed. We had another discussion about selling *Madi*; she was too expensive to maintain and we needed to build our savings back up. The market had also changed. We wouldn't get half what we paid for her but we decided I would go back and prepare her for the market. I needed familiarity and I needed to get my head on straight. So I packed a few things and went to live aboard *Madi*. It felt right. It not only saved my life; it changed my perception of it forever.

# 26

# VENICE: WHEN TIME FELT PURE AND PRESENT

2010

∾

I t was hard to find fault with our new home. Colette and Godot loved being back in the small scale space aboard *Madi* and she was located less than an hour from Venice. In less than a year the country had changed along with the pressures that came with it. In Geneva, it mattered a great deal that I was out of work and homeless; here, not so much. If Muv couldn't offer periodic assurances, I would just have to settle for Mother Nature. She was everywhere and very much alive. Her force was powerful and carried enough authority to wipe away any confusion I felt about the future. She washed away the tension and cleansed the mind. My new home was furnished with familiar items, including my books, where I could embrace the environs and enjoy my last gasp of *Madi*. As they say: "The two best days in a sailor's life are the day they buy the boat and the day they sell it".

As far as I was concerned there were two projects to complete. The first was to get our boat into ship shape and the second was to make sure I followed her lead. From the moment I moved aboard *Madi* there was the promise of transformation. I wanted to like myself again, and find some inner peace. This was of vital importance, and like my attitude, *Madi*'s bright work was in desperate need of attention. Most days were spent sanding, scrubbing, and varnishing her railings. The cockpit required a lot of work and eventually she received an entire new coat on her teak deck. *Madi* got the full treatment and I even had her hauled her out of the water so she could receive a proper scrub underneath.

I moved from winter in Geneva to spring in Lignano and the weather was only going to get better. I began to feel rejuvenated for two reasons; I had serious work and it felt like I was making progress. After a full day's work I sat aft deck with Colette and Godot at my feet and began the exercise of repairing myself. As she had in the past, Italy acted as a balm, and she was ready to do it once again. There was no reason to compete with her because she was more of a hedonist than I could ever be and the world often looks most attractive when viewing her from a boat. Especially when it's stationary.

I bought a collapsible bike with a basket for Colette and Godot in the front, and room to store groceries in the back. I cycled off the dock in the late afternoon and it took less than twenty minutes to reach the small town. We three cycled beneath the pine trees lining the streets, and passed along the beaches full of golden sand. The lavish parks before us were packed with recreational areas designated for camping. The smell of pine was intense and everywhere. Being broke wasn't all that bad, especially when I had a teak salon to hang out in; I was starting to embrace life again.

Sometimes I took the dogs for a walk along the boardwalk and found a favorite bar to drink the aperitif called

Aperol. This cocktail came with an orange flavored mixer because it was Italy, a beloved color, but it was created in a myriad of ways. Either a splash of still water or maybe sparkling, a local wine, or something semi-sweet or a little dry. Often it came with a couple ice cubes but there was always a slice of orange inside.

I wasn't a fan of the bitter cocktails Italians prefer to drink before dinner to whet their appetite, yet I loved their Aperol, but never could hang out like the locals. After an hour or two I admitted defeat and cycled home, but this was a sweet defeat.

If I desired company it was remedied by listening to podcasts. They were on the rise and available at any hour. I chose two and they became the most popular in the following decade. Marc Maron and Alex Jones; each sat directly opposite the other, culturally and politically. They were uniquely miserable in their own way. Jones pined for the past whereas Maron was waiting impatiently for the future. Jones, the right wing guy, came with conspiracy laced ideas and Maron was perpetually gripped by self-analysis, forever anxious to get to the root of his problem. If social media was becoming the distraction there was still time for the long form podcast. I had plenty of time and these voices each carried their own force.

Both went on rants. Jones was a hardcore salesman, a modern day Elmer Gantry without a heart, whereas Maron had a pulse. The latter didn't play at being a preacher, instead, Maron was a fanboy, an emotional guy who was genuinely interested in his guests. Together they told me everything I needed to know about the temperature of home. I was curious to know how pathologies were playing out and while listening to both ends of the spectrum it sounded as if intense polarization was gaining traction in my former home.

My own misery was fading away because I wasn't insisting that it leave immediately. I still missed Muv a great deal but that was natural. What disappointed me most was that she never came back in my dreams. I decided I wasn't ready to assimilate her spirit because I wasn't healthy. First came the body, then the mind could follow in its footsteps. I gave myself six months to address the challenge, six months until the Bora winds arrived. My daily diet was an exercise in routine which I dearly missed. Lunch came with salads filled with shrimp or eggs, some bread, butter and jam, and plenty of water throughout the day. At night I tucked into the galley and prepared a piece of fish or a slice of meat, and because *Madi* was no longer at sea, she was no longer dry— there were bottles of various red and local white wine available on board.

Francis stayed with us on the weekend and a friend or two flew in from Seattle to make sure I hadn't fallen off the face of the earth. Oddly enough I was beginning to feel more centered than ever. Initially it was hard to be alone until it felt okay and then I learned to enjoy it. Life was simple but it was surprising the amount of choices I still had to make. Nights were quiet and *Madi* was full of books although the the majority of my time was spent re-visiting Gore Vidal and Dawn Powell. I probably got to know more about my country's history and politics through his prescient essays than I ever did while living there; there was a reason Vidal's four favorite words were "I told you so."

I never took *Madi* outside the marina and we were both fine with that fact. I got down to the basics and reviewed everything I used because that's what one does on a boat. I focused on the vital elements, and Mother Nature was always there, in the foreground, tapping her fingers and waiting for me to understand what I did with my rubbish and why I created so much of it in the first place. The idea of purchasing anything new other than my bike and groceries felt frivolous. If disposable cash had been available, which it wasn't, I was less inclined to dispose of the little I had without great internal debate. Existing in this limbo state felt somehow essential before I could move forward with any confidence. It grew impossible to dwell on particulars outside of my immediate lifestyle. There was my routine and there were my two projects. And then there was Venice.

Kenneth Tynan, the wittiest of British critics, once wrote: "What, when drunk, one sees in other women, we see in Garbo, sober." This was applicable to Venice. Sometime I went by train, other times by car. The minute land disappeared, and the eyes caught sight of the lagoon, everything else evaporates. One is instantaneously pulled into her astounding sense of glamour. Even her public transport felt exotic. In a city with less than 30,000 residents, packed with people who talk of nothing but real estate, destinations were readily found.

My friend Elise educated me on their holy topic, real estate, and she also helped manage the marina. Elise lived nearby with her family and visited our boat every now and then, making sure I hadn't fallen overboard. Elise was uniquely appreciated because she let me view Venice through the local eye. She picked me up at the marina and we drove to Venice in less than an hour. Sometimes we wandered down narrow alleys until we found some hole in the wall. Once inside we received a warm greeting, followed by some red wine served from brightly colored ceramic carafes. If Francis came along we would all linger at the bar consuming the light and fluffy pastry called polpetta until it was time to escape further into the labyrinth of alleys to our final destination: her friend's restaurant. I never could have found it on my own due to my poor sense of direction.

It was charming and the setting so deceptively simple with tables sans linen, and light, white cotton curtains covering little square windows. There were no strangers, only me. We stood at the bar, drinking the white wine the region is known for, eating small slices of white bread covered in creamy mild codfish called Baccala. Older men lined up the bar, replaced by younger ones as the sun set outside, while the voluptuous bartender from Bologna entertained us.

"How did you end up here?" I asked.

She laughed, "I don't know, the plan was to stay a month and I never left."

Elise left Francis and I at the bar but I kept an eye on her silhouette. She sat in the kitchen on a wooden table, gossiping with friends as cooks and waiters erased her image every few minutes. Then she jumped off, came back to us and announced it was time to sit down for dinner. We congregated at a small table and Chef Claudio came over to explain the choices. Several items were discussed at length as he took our temperature, gaging the precise mood. Appetizers came and went along with the black squid pasta until it was finally time for dessert. So small and simple but that dark chocolate tort filled with warm chocolate sauce satiated every part of my body. If happiness wasn't my goal it was unavoidable on that night.

Past midnight, finally time for the local gossip, it was understood Claudio must be the narrator so we waited until he sat down with a glass of red wine. He began and it went something like this: a trio of kids from Padova arrived for a night out on the town. They were not the brightest and they proceeded to get very drunk. Two of them decided the third must go back, get their car, drive into the city in order to take them home. It's a dare and it must be done. Improbably, the third kid managed to navigate his car across two bridges, including Ponte dell'Accademia', the one with all those steps before the polizia caught up with him. He was so scared he threw the car keys into the canal, as if this would suggest he hadn't been driving. Those precious keys could not be retrieved quickly, and it took all night, and a barge to get the car removed from the bridge. The following day the mother placed a full-page ad in the local newspaper, *Il Gazattino,* which read: "Our family would like to apologize to the citizens of Venice for the stupidity of my son." Even their gossip had a flair all its own.

There were plenty of smart young men around town. One night I saw a beautiful boy with laurels in his hair; he looked slightly inebriated. I asked Francis about it and he said, "They wear the traditional *Laurea* when they've earned their master's degree."

I walked up to the beautiful boy and asked, "Congratulations, what did you get your degree in?"

He responded nonchalantly, "Architecture, of course."

I was always distracted by the slightest item in Venice. For instance, if I walked across a bridge I might stop because my eyes land on a small bright cobalt blue boat tied up, floating below a window. Maybe a couple of potted plants precariously lined up on the ledge beneath the glass, full of rosemary or sage or some red tulips. Below the window there might be some laundry dangling, just one or two pieces of cloth, nothing spectacular. It's the kind of scene offered at any port town, perhaps, but my eyes lose focus when I step back. Then I take another and the portrait explodes as the simplest picture has become a masterpiece in La Serenissima.

It was irrelevant how many canals I drifted down in my past, because drifting down Venetian canals, on a vaporetto at night was like a movie set. It was atmospheric, I could barely make out the inhabitants going about their business, yet I was a keen voyeur. To catch them at a small table, as they ate, or read a book or watched television on an old couch—they are in their palazzi and I am transported to another era.

One trip, in particular, was taken more than once, when I felt the gripping need to pay homage to Sergei Diaghilev and his grave at Isola di San Michele. I had become slightly obsessed with cemeteries in Italy. It's where my fetish for flowers was fed while each grave provided a snapshot into the lives of the deceased. Their photographs were carved into stone; grainy, romantic black and white photos representing the person beneath the ground. There is nothing, really, to compare to the grand cemetery in Genoa, covered in hundreds of majestic statues, but San Michele comes close. This cemetery has splendor and is worth a trip to San Michele on its own.

Diaghilev's grave is located in the Orthodox section, near the composer Igor Stravinsky, with whom he collaborated. On Diaghilev's I noticed stones left in the middle, on the shelf of his elaborate structure, with notes carefully written and left below. It's predictably unique, a tall white marble structure with a dome on top. I imagined all the ballet dancers and artists who came to pay tribute. Diaghilev's reign at Ballet Russes was epic, literally; during the epoch period. I thought of all those well known names who followed their maestro through European tours, and how he introduced the East to the West through ballet. It was obvious why Picasso and Cocteau, Stravinsky and Nijinsky, and even Brecht followed him all over Europe. Why the Italian painter Giorgio de Chirico, and the designer Chanel wanted to create his scenery and design his costumes. Why Ravel, Rubinstein, and all the rest followed Diaghilev wherever he went. He created magic at every stop along the way. Diaghilev, the Russian, the failed composer and father of modern art. He had one desire and that wish was to die in Venice. I thought about Muv and the ballet and smiled as we took the vaporetto back to land.

I continued to cycle underneath the pine trees during the day and read Gore Vidal's essays at night. Sometimes I fantasized about how our lives overlapped. Vidal lived in southern Italy and I gravitated towards the north. When we lived in Rome I used to take road trips down south, drive through Positano and then further down to Ravello. I walked by his splendid Villa La Rondinaia several times but wouldn't dare knock on his door. Once I ate at the restaurant he frequented but the goal was never to meet my idol. I just wanted to remember my country through his essays. It was good enough to feel like we were sitting across from one another, in high backed chairs, drinking a glass of Chivas. I knew one or two people that knew him but why would I ever want to puncture the tranquil picture that existed in my mind. His essays were like a bible and if I ever missed America all I had to do was pick up one of his books. He was my teacher and Italy was a gift.

Then summer drifted away and the weather began to shift. The wicked Bora winds approached and once they came onto the dock they rocked the boat so hard, even *Madi* couldn't resist their power. Mother Nature was kind and she was also there to remind me it was time to go because I couldn't live next to La Serenissima forever.

I lined up potential buyers but her new owner had yet to land on one of my ads. The project in Geneva was about to end and a new project in Kazakhstan was about to begin for Francis. I wasn't going to move there so we decided on Amsterdam. It was another international city, like Geneva, geared towards expats. We had enough cash to get our stuff out of storage and put down first and last month's rent. It was time for Amsterdam, and I was ready.

# 27

## AMSTERDAM: WHEN TIME FELT
## RECYCLED

~

I f Paris and Edinburgh had an affair their love child would look like Amsterdam. Canals lined with savvy and kinky shops and services safely contained within a handsome, brooding exterior. And the citizens would be good looking and very tall; this last quality, quintessentially Dutch, came across like an unexpected perk. Short people can be annoying, while tall people, in general, are often not.

This was illustrated one beautiful day in early spring. It wasn't raining as I walked along one of the main canals called Prinsengracht. A Dutch couple approached from afar, even at a distance of ten meters, they appear very tall. They were both around thirty years old and held hands in a relaxed fashion. Each opted for a smart overcoat, his was charcoal, hers dove grey, unbuttoned. Both were made of wool gabardine and worn right above the knee. Each had on a pair of black wool slacks with sleek creases, dark leather shoes beneath, flat, not too shiny with tips not too sharp. Far above, the man's brown hair was slicked back, making it look almost black, a common look, a little wavy at the base covering the back of his white collar. His button-down shirt was neatly tucked beneath a dark brown wool sweater and I don't think he was wearing a tie but my attention was drawn to the woman's long, perfectly straight hair. It had to be admired, flowing gently away from her face, with natural blonde highlights and skin that was pale and pristine; she looked shy.

As they approached it became apparent each had a matching set of large hazel colored eyes. Her silk cream blouse hung below her beige cashmere sweater, a v-neck and very stylish. Both of their long bodies were in fine shape, faces slightly chiseled, they could have been twins if they weren't so deeply in love. I assumed their engagement was recent, that their wedding would be intimate, surrounded by close family and friends and they will live happily ever after.

I was lost in their bliss and forgot to move aside. Sidewalk etiquette is practiced in Amsterdam, say, unlike Paris, where the worst offenders are men. But here, along the canal, I was too captivated by their love story. I stood about 5'10" in my boots and they towered over me, each well over six feet, and he closer to seven. Two gentle giants without any need for attention because they receive it just by walking along the canal. A couple that restored my faith in mankind. Right before our collision, the very second before I could smell their peppermint breath, their hands released and parted like the Red Sea. I looked back, already missing them, wishing it could happen all over again. I was so happy I laughed out loud. The rest of my day was dull.

Living in Amsterdam affirmed all that is fine and dandy, how life can be cool and comfortable, not unlike the handsome couple. The environs were stable and constantly aimed towards sensibility and civility. Most of the natives have business savvy baked into their DNA. There was more than a whiff of Seattle in the air due to industrious behavior, and the rain and grey skies reminded me of home.

I had landed in a country of merchants. The historical indicators leered down on Amsterdam's three major canals; Prinsengracht, Herengracht, and then Keisersgracht. All I had to do was look up at the triangular roofs with their quaint gables and note the large, distinctive black hooks once used to hang the bulky items transported from port to their 'warehouse'. These people knew how to trade with the outside world because they had been doing it effectively for centuries. The concept of trade flowed through their veins. It was second nature to secure a contract agreeable to all parties—it's done out of necessity, executed in this fashion for a very long time.

Some of our reference points overlapped because they could be nostalgic about America's Kennedy era. This meant my relationship with Holland began on familiar terms. It was as trendy as any place in Europe, and the Dutch are devoted fans of both England and America; their culture as current as any on the continent. They could have been England's only true fan in Europe if it weren't for the Danes.

This helped to eliminate much of the low level stress I'd felt in other foreign countries but morphed into another kind of mental challenge. As if suggesting I stay attached to a former self, a former a la mode lifestyle. It came across so familiar it could make me uncomfortable like time had been recycled, like I'd been transported back to Seattle surrounded by young hipsters and multi-national corporations. If they were trendy in Europe they were just catching up to North America.

I got into a routine and walked by a Pilates studio every day. I explored the idea of getting certified, of becoming an instructor. I'd probably been doing it longer than anyone around here but then I'd have to learn Dutch and that would be a bridge too far. I couldn't imagine conquering that sound that made German seem lyrical. I couldn't even pronounce the name of the street we lived on; Voetboogstraat; it hurt the back of my throat and strained the vocal chords. I once tried to justify this complaint at lunch with a couple of Dutch professionals, one from Arthur Anderson and very pragmatic. She accepted my observation then dismissed it.

She said, "Yes, I guess the G can be harsh, but you should listen to the Queen, she really knows how to soften it."

If I couldn't pronounce Voetboogstraat it didn't decrease the happiness felt living on it. This street boasted the finest made Belgian french fries. It was located at number thirty-three, only a few doors down from our own. A little square hole in the wall, literally, called Vlaam's Friteshuis Vleminckx, large enough to fit two people and a couple of ovens to fry the potatoes. Large, light, crispy fries, salted to perfection. We're encouraged to eat them with mayonnaise, or with ketchup and this is heaven. As Woody Allen once said, Protestants remain on intimate terms with both mayonnaise and WonderBread.

Each country in which I lived was stamped with its own sense of time. In Rome, it felt like it stopped. In Paris, it flew by, then halted so fast I went into a state of panic. In Malta, time felt lost. In Lignano Sabbiadoro I was present. Yet Amsterdam threw me back into the past. I'd become more introspective and increasingly less interested in the social scene as I skidded into my forties; I was starting to feel some anxiety. Living in Lignano had changed me forever. I no longer fed off social activity; it was feeding on me, and maybe it always had. Anyway, if familiarity didn't breed contempt here in Amsterdam, it sure could made life feel boring at times.

One afternoon was spent hanging out with a Dutch guy named Hans who'd been a good friend of mine since Paris. I was quizzing him about his tribe over lunch one day. He said, without any need to be defensive, "We're one dimensional, there's no need to analyze us."

After Italy I assumed most tribes were complicated and worthy of inspection. But he was right and not the first one to say it. Historically, one could argue they were German, and once upon a time part of the German tribe. They'll never admit that yet there's no denying the very specific connection to Germany's economy; they often spoke German due to this important, if inconspicuous reliance on their neighbor. There is a strong sense of solidarity between the EU members but Holland is a country of merchants whereas Germany is full of engineers. I doubt any other tribe could have absorbed East Germany in such a short time and with so much success.

I had traveled to Berlin several times, and Munich, in fact I'd driven through most of Germany and Austria. I also spent time at the family flat on Lake Garda, a building owned by as many Germans as Italians. I was beginning to think my idea of living in Germany, after Rome and Paris, wouldn't have matched the fantasy created in my mind. They could be awfully rigid. They are extraordinarily disciplined, intent on putting their past behind them and focused on the future, completely; this is precisely why they have become the biggest exporter on the planet. But I was beginning to think I hadn't missed out by not living in Germany.

The Dutch do have specific talents. They have superior knowledge managing dykes and water. Venice might want to take advantage and follow suit, however, getting the rest of Italy to invest so much money into a problem uniquely their own, remained the central issue. During my year long stay in Amsterdam I met a historian who was curious about my time in Venice. After taking a few mental notes she said with a shrug, "Well, if we had the Gondolas and Gondoliers we could be just like Venice." It made me laugh because her comment provided a window into her attitude towards nuance, not to mention quintessential Dutch behavior.

But I always felt lucky in geography and with the company experienced in Amsterdam. Like Seattle, it was an incredibly livable city, anyone could adapt if they tried. I became friends with a few Dutch guys who worked with Francis on his project in Kazakhstan. As I said, they can work with anyone, anywhere. They are solid, smart and steady and their confidence is admirable. They too are perpetually focused on the future and trade.

And the Dutch loved a good party. They floated happily down their canals on a sunny day with a smile on their face, a Heineken in one hand, the universal thumbs up sign on the other as they posed for selfies. They can also be cheap. Prosecco may not be Champagne but they called it their 'bubbly'. It was economical and showed up at more than one party. When Hans threw his New Year's bash there was plenty of bubbly and great wine and we partied into the next year overlooking the canal on Prinsengracht. Just after midnight a middle aged man fell down. I assumed he might have suffered a small heart attack. I thought someone should call an ambulance but no one got excited in this crowd. After about twenty minutes, he got off the couch and continued with the festivities. It's hard to rattle a Dutchman, especially when they're flying high on Prosecco.

When it was time to have my wisdom teeth out I made the appointment down the street at the dentist's office and after the procedure I assumed a painkiller might be prescribed; after all they had just exposed a nerve. No such luck, as I paid at the window the woman took my money, then sighed, handed me two Paracetamol, and made a gesture towards the exit door. I went home, ate a brownie and suffered the consequences. It was the only time I felt perturbed.

When Francis and I went to get our annual blood tests, Francis left and I stayed for a breast exam. I got chatty with the doctor and eventually he got chatty back. He said, "You aren't the typical expat. You know, some of them come into my office and put a small baggie on my desk insisting I fill all the prescriptions, it's amazing, an entire bag." He shook his head in amazement.

But like I said, I did buy a brownie every now and then. Never a huge fan of smoking pot, however, when in Rome, as they say....

However, I never knew anyone else who did drugs, and for all their legalized prostitution and coffee houses and massive selection of drugs; the Dutch are inherently conservative. The tourist attractions are generally relegated to tourists and provide plenty of trade.

I missed great food, or rather, I missed good value for great food. Their television carried the same competitive food programs and the town had some terrific international restaurants but after you've hit the European joints who wants to eat Indonesian every night? Their grocery stores were less than spectacular but if you wanted to pay for it, and I did, there was a store within walking distance offering an excellent selection. It was just a very expensive choice. When I couldn't take it any longer, we went to Brussels. It took two and a half hours and it was worth the drive because the Belgians are deeply serious about food; in fact the French hop a train to Brussels when in need of a truly unique gastronomic experience. Like the Dutch, the Belgians are serious about business and negotiations, unlike the Dutch, this includes food too.

Amsterdam was a navigable city with convenient transport and trams to any destination within the city. I took a test drive on their bicycles but found them too large and slightly unyielding. If you kept pedaling forward you were fine but there was little room for finesse. There is no doubt the Dutch cyclist gets right away over pedestrians every time. I tried to take Colette and Godot for a ride but their bikes don't accommodate baskets. Instead they offered me a large orange cart. The cart sat at the back, it was square and deep and the dogs looked lost. We didn't go far because the carts are meant for parents to put their children in the back; they are meant to train kids to be tough. Instead of putting plastic over their heads when the weather gets rough they let the plastic covers flip wide open so the young ones can brave the elements, making sure they are strong and resilient by the age of five.

Amsterdam had a couple of fantastic museums but I couldn't find my favorite Van Gogh called "Cafe Terraces at Midnight". So I took the train to Otterlo, a small suburban village outside of Amsterdam. It was refreshing to get out of the trendy city and find where the families lived and the houses they lived in. Most were classic and compact, elegant, without much fuss.

The museum was five kilometers away so bicycles were

still necessary and available for transport. I took one and ventured deep inside the National Park De Hoge Veluwe at the Kroller-Muller Museum. I found my Van Gogh alongside plenty of other masters, including Monet, Picasso, Seurat, Braque, and Cezanne.

I did make time to send out my resume. I didn't get a recruiting job but came close. I was called in for a serious management position at a large company but an offer wasn't extended. Once again I couldn't close the deal. This didn't stop them from asking me to come in a few more times. It felt like deja vu, but then so did everything else in Amsterdam. I suppose the idea of doing what I'd done in Seattle felt like moving backwards. It didn't stop them from bringing me in for more interviews but we both remained on the fence.

I had a few dinner parties and through one of my contacts I managed to land a job for a slick magazine based out of Istanbul. I wrote some articles about some interesting people I'd met along my travels and it got me writing on a regular basis. It didn't pay much, but it was enough because the project Francis had with the Kazakhs was expanding into a large company. He was back on his feet financially.

If I craved an emotional experience all I had to do was walk two blocks east of our flat and find "Ann Frank's Museum". It was a three-story canal house located at Prinsengracht 263. A secret annex to the past, where visitors could watch the most famous diary unfold before their very eyes. By the time we'd reached the first floor, a desperately intense life comes back to haunt us all. Following her journey to the bitter end, every item penetrates the senses, including the 3 x 5 cards kept so meticulously by the Germans, along with the vague video clips. With little space we watched chapters of the story unwind on the walls in little fold out chairs. I didn't think about my trip to Auschwitz because there's only one victim and that was the little girl named Ann Frank who lived on Prinsengracht 263.

If I craved flowers we went to Keukenhof Gardens, known as the Garden of Europe. One of the largest flower gardens in the world, situated in Lisse, in Southern Holland. There's about seven million flower bulbs planted annually covering about thirty-two hectares and if anyone doubts the Dutch and their ability to cultivate all they have to do is witness the tulips at Keukenhof Gardens.

Our flat was located in the center of town, next to the flower market where I could feed my fetish for flowers on a weekly basis, and outside our front door lived one of the best book markets in the world. Every Friday morning I went downstairs and spent the morning browsing old, rare, and second hand books at Spui Square. Books from dozens of booksellers, books about everything for any kind of connoisseur or dilettante. Every subject was covered in English, Dutch, French, and German along with pamphlets, posters, documents, and periodicals from across the planet.

Overlooking the market lived cafe culture at his best at the Luxembourg Cafe. I had become a bit of a loner but I had enough friends to enjoy a glass of wine with, and watch the world go by. The Populist movement was on the march with Geert Wilders, the peroxide blonde guy, he who would gravely portend future politics on the continent as well as across the pond. I watched and waited. Life was fine and steady in Amsterdam but the world was conspiring for us to leave, or specifically, a Dutch bank suggested we might want to move. Not from the city, just from our apartment.

All of our documentation was in order and it had been easy to get residency within the first month of our arrival. We banked in Holland, we paid our rent each month, on time, unfortunately our landlord failed to inform us she had foreclosed on her mortgage. She was an American who moved back to the States shortly after buying the flat. Unlike my other landlords, she never wanted to speak over the phone, allowing only two or three email exchanges. It was unusual but I never expected a visit from her bank. I had used a real estate company in the same way I had in previous cities but the blame couldn't be placed on our agent. It certainly wasn't our fault but it was now our problem.

When the banker showed up at our front door he didn't threaten us, he wasn't going to kick us out, and he could see we weren't the type to squat. Our friend Hans recommended a Dutch attorney who was open minded but advised we move out.

For us, the most obvious choice was to move to another country. Our time had come full circle because we had spent about a year in Amsterdam. Francis, once again, was immersed in another start up but this one came with large oil sales and it was expanding. He was starting to divide his time between Kazakhstan and Romania, recruiting engineers. Kazakhstan had oil, gas and money but they lacked talent. Francis suggested we move to Prague. He had never lived in Central Europe, and my imagination didn't stretch that far, but this didn't stop me from exploring bohemian ideals including truth, love and beauty.

Above all, I was beginning to assimilate Muv and I specifically remember the moment it started to happen. She didn't come back in my dreams, but appeared in lessons still needed to be learned. She had probably tried to teach me these by example while she was still alive, when I wasn't receptive. The lessons were often attached to altering my perspective, bending the mind, opening it to the idea of being present. She was probably hanging around Lignano Sabbiadoro the entire time.

Then one day she decided to visit while I was on a long distant drive crossing Europe's borders. I had to address an issue at the flat on Lake Garda. I never liked to fly and preferred the car, because of Colette and Godot, especially if it entailed a journey through Europe. I took plenty of trains but as an American the exercise of driving felt essential. The long cruise was picturesque and uneventful until I entered the long stretch of tunnels guiding me from France to Italy. I stopped looking at the scenery because I was overcome by Muv's presence; or was it her essence; either way, she was everywhere.

I looked around and said out loud, "Muv?" I looked outside the windows, then I glanced at the dogs laying across the passenger seat. I wouldn't have been shocked to see Muv materialize with Colette and Godot on her lap. She wasn't there, of course, she only occupied all the air. She permeated every part of my body. There was no discomfort or confusion, instead, I just felt deeply at peace. I've no idea what was going inside my head, and it only lasted for a few minutes. Then she left in the same way she arrived; like a breath of fresh air. I felt loved, as before, and everything was going to be fine. Amsterdam had been a terrific pit stop and now I was off to explore my Bohemian ideals in Prague.

# 28

# PRAGUE: WHEN TIME OPENED UP
## 2011-2012

~

Francis considered Prague a romantic as well as pragmatic choice because the airport offered direct flights to Kazakhstan. He was shuttling back and forth with greater frequency and it wasn't the first time direct flights played a role in our destination. His project was expanding fast and he was starting to split his time between Bucharest and Kazakhstan.

I too considered Prague romantic and heard her whispering sweet things into my ear, like a subliminal mantra, daring me to let go of my bourgeoisie past. My mind opened up and became fanciful. Prague offered a stage on which I could chase Bohemian ideals because they weren't restricted to painters and poets. Our nomadic lifestyle had become unconventional so it wasn't that much of a stretch. Why not be a poser or at least sit across from one in a deep purple velvet jacket drinking absinthe at the Cafe Royal? I was comfortable doing this at Cafe de Flore on boulevard Saint-Germain in Paris.

Prague elevated this idea and teased that I might find "men in monocles, along with the kohl-eyed beauties in chiffon and emeralds," as Virginia Nicholson suggested. She was probably channeling the Bloomsbury set although this attitude was available to anyone living anywhere; a *curioso* just had to create their own if they couldn't find it downtown. The more I thought about it the more this fantasy lit up like a wildfire after the practical qualities of Holland. Yes, I agreed, Prague should be our next city.

Preparation was key so I engaged in the necessary research for transplanting our lives once again. This exercise had become rote. At first it looked like a puzzle, until neighborhoods were studied, and blogs written by expats, discovered and read. The usual suspects were reviewed until the right real estate agent came forward. This time it was an American woman who had been living in the Czech Republic for decades. I flew to Prague and we looked at several rentals in a couple of neighborhoods. I was relieved at its affordability. When I got back to Amsterdam I called the moving company and started comparing prices. I waited for the quotes to arrive in my inbox and began to pack.

It didn't take long to find an ideal flat in a leafy neighborhood called Vinohrady that fit our budget. Two large bedrooms with one operating as an office. Two bathrooms were key to any marriage and this one also boasted a large kitchen and one very spacious salon with beautifully carved double doors and the highest ceiling I had ever seen. It reminded me of Audrey Hepburn's flat in 'Charade'. Another set of doors took us out to a large ornate balcony with gargoyles glaring down from either side. The view didn't show off her landmarks but there were a few gothic churches and grand architecture on the one side with a train track splitting the view into two. A picturesque and bohemian version of Mona Lisa, with one side representing the city's past, abundant with trees and parks, the other offering a modern industrial reality. We were close to the city center and within minutes I could find stores to buy groceries, items to hang the paintings, power supplies, and necessities required to make our move appear seamless, if only to me.

*...a bank and Bohemia*

WE CHOSE a bank and it was insane. The fact we didn't have much money was irrelevant; just walking into the financial institution felt palatial. Actually, once it had been a palace, before it became a museum, then, perhaps a theater. Moving east was beginning to feel delightfully abstract as it unlocked the imagination, especially a bank that looked like Ceska Sporitelna.

We chose the old institution for its terrific expat services geared toward short term residents. It was a glorious reflection of an Austrian Hungarian past built in a grand Neo-Renaissance style boasting the kind of interior I'd never seen in a building as mundane as a bank. The lobby was opulent with a striking staircase and high walls on either side, creating a tunnel-like effect with black iron gates, and goddesses standing at the bottom. Polished red granite pillars encased in pale brown and gold paintwork made the ascent to the upper story feel surreal.

The top floor mesmerized the eyes with a vast series of murals covering the entire ceiling. The overall impact was extraordinarily impressive even if our bank accounts held

just enough to cover monthly expenses. The Polivka's archi-
tectural style had spectacular historicism. Art nouveau
exploded all over the city but this was our bank and I could
visit on a regular basis. When I asked for a deposit box they
guided me downstairs into a smaller room with rows of
ornate drawers, ancient and slim beige boxes gilded with
elegant design and carefully preserved. I received deposit
box #1. We finally sold *Madi* and Francis gave me half, or
rather I insisted on it as money seemed to fall through his
fingers. I exchanged my fiat currency for gold coins bought
at an Austrian bank and figured the next time we were
broke I could retrieve my little stash.

Expectations were exceeded on a weekly basis in Prague.
A neighborhood store confirmed suspicions that elusive
Bohemian ideals might be hidden behind patterns of
another kind. I found a retailer where I could mix my own
elixir of scents and oils with various olive oils, specialty
liqueurs, brandies, and whiskies of all kinds. After making a
purchase the young saleswoman wrote the name in cursive
with a large white pencil on the artisan styled clear bottles.

Prague was a separate entity. Just buying a bottle of
brandy felt creative. I couldn't think of an Anglo Saxon
equivalent. The task became less about taking in tourist
attractions and more about imbibing the mystical aspects of
our new home. I could breathe better, think better and let
my imagination run wild. Amsterdam could feel like
London with everyone stuffed into the city, existing on top
of one another like ants. In Paris, careful navigation was
often necessary, even in Malta, a tiny island, traffic jams
were a constant. In Prague, like Rome, there was plenty of
blessed space. This enhanced the notion I might discover a
few of my own ideals.

The architecture was reminiscent of Rome mixed in

with some regal Austrian-Habsburg aspects; as pretty as
Paris, without so many distractions. Her features were fetch-
ing, even sweet, when balanced out by the reality of living
side by side with the Slavs. They were Slavs but specifically
unique from the Russians, Balkans, Slovakians, and Belaru-
sians. On the surface they were civil and kept to their own
business. They engaged in the world, wearing a veil of
mystery, allowing them to maintain just enough distance.

They were also cold. If I threw a smile their way, I didn't
expect it would be sent back. So I just let the interior of the
city give me clues to a personality as I walked along her
long, broad, inviting boulevards, cutting through vast parks
and statues floating everywhere, like goddesses protecting
their city, applying a sympathetic vibe.

Her famous cafe culture was very much alive. It was
whimsical, then severe, with lighting more elaborate, often
more elegant, than what I'd seen in Austria. Once upon a
time they occupied a small slice of her empire. However, the
Czechs could resemble the Hungarians who were the only
country with a non-Indo European language. And they were
stubborn, like the Hungarians, when faced with globalization. Prague's personality was scribbled all over their faces;
crystal blue eyes set far apart, aimed straight ahead, below
wide chiseled cheek bones, almost flat without ever so much
as a glance when I stared at them on the street. If they were
pretty, they took my breath away, but they kept up an attitude of resistance towards the modern world of branding.

If they were disappointed in how much their society had
succumbed to commercialization, the opposite came across,
but then my entire life had been saturated in marketing
since I was a child. Even when a large ad was on full display
over a bridge, or splattered across a building, the message
faded into the background. I didn't see the effects of adver-

tising on their backs, or on their feet, or attached to a hand-bag. It still felt like an afterthought. Maybe they just knew how to dial it down. It reminded me of Fellini's Italy in the 60's when the Italians led a fierce, albeit short lived rebellion against America's Madison Avenue hard core sell. I responded to this enthusiastically because I was heading in the opposite direction. Long live the resistance.

Moving east had been the right decision, contrary to what other people might think, including a Dutch woman I met in a wine shop. We were standing next to one another at a wine tasting. While sipping my Pinot Grigio I said, "I'm moving to Prague next month."

She turned her glance my way and looked me up and down. "Oh, you're moving east, I've no idea why."

I was slightly offended, feeling a little defensive, until I suspected she probably had never been outside Paris and London. I kept my concerns private, knowing my odyssey struck others as odd, even weird. It was a road less traveled and I could understand how it raised a couple of eyebrows. I was hoping to wind it down but how? The only thing I knew at the time was Prague, like Paris, was a finite proposition.

# 29

# A GATEWAY

~

T hen I read a book by Daniela Hodrova called, *Prague, I See a City*. Ms. Hodrova wrote about a monk named Cosmas who playfully suggested the city's name derived from the Slavonic word for 'threshold'. Cosmas ordained his city would always be in torment, yet this notion of Prague as a threshold carried a far more positive connotation for me. It served my philosophy that the chalice could be within reach and Prague could offer a gateway.

To what or where, I still wasn't sure, because travel remained a constant condition. Either in the mind, by sky, train, or by automobile I continued to move forward while others assumed it might be the other way around. I often asked myself whether I was escaping from, or heading towards a fixed destination. The answer was ambivalent and I always fell back on Muv's confidence I would eventually figure it out and land on my feet. When I was young and struggling through those painful months following the birth of my child, she chose to rely on the rare cliché, and said, "I suppose it's true what they say that the shortest route home is always the longest."

~

*...Another death*

~

EVERYDAY PROVIDED me with a new normal. My brother sent me a curt email the day after my father's death. I shared this message with Francis which inspired a spontaneous sharp intake of breathe, "Oh!"

But I wasn't surprised by this brother's actions because they were always consistent. His email didn't have the ability to shock because I had already mourned my father's passing from my life and suspected the end was near. The last time we spoke was on my birthday the previous year. It was an unbearably sad conversation. In the past my parents would call me on my birthday and sing me the birthday song over the phone and then we'd laugh. This time he didn't even bother to mention my anniversary and dove right in, "You have to stop writing because your mother is outside the corridor and she's pacing, and it's upsetting her."

My father had never been aggressive, it wasn't in his nature, so I responded gently, "But Dad, Mother died, you remember, right?"

He became agitated and said he knew she was dead and then he repeated his concern. We went through another cycle and he hung up the phone only to call right back. As I listened to him I remembered how I used to write short stories when I was ten years old. My family found them amusing and they piled up in the closet until I had several piles over four feet high. One day, when I was out, my father put them on the patio and the rain destroyed them all. I didn't get mad because I believed he was just trying to clean out my closet. But now I began to wonder and decided to pass the phone to Francis. My father became his old self; kind, inquiring. The call ended and Francis shrugged his shoulders in confusion. He tried calling back and we decided not to pick up the phone.

His dementia and the geographical distance were a deadly combination on our relationship. I knew he didn't want anyone to know about the affair; I understood the call was about our relationship. It had nothing to do with Muv, and yet it had everything to do with his wife and her relationship to me. I had loved him for a lifetime and we shared genuine affection with a lot of laughter. He was kind, a good father, and a decent man. It was easy to ascertain family members had made their way into his brain. He probably welcomed it. He had always been fragile and now he was weak and dementia was cruel. I had heard some things from my family in California because, as they say, there are always witnesses. It was easier to recall the good times because there had been so many and I was sad but did not shed any tears because he was finally at peace.

*...discovering my Bohemian Ideals with The Pirate Party*

PRAGUE WAS a safe and sensible place to hear such news. She wasn't overtly emotional and she could be gentle on the senses. I stayed away from tourist traps allowing my daily excursions to guide me off the beaten path. This let residents come into sharper focus. One day I stopped to watch two older women standing at the bus stop from across the street. Their hands stranded in mid air, cupping their ears as if to keep the rest of the world away. Engaged, with great affection in their eyes, smiling, leaning into one another. Both were bulky, unfashionable, wearing hats they'd worn for decades. There was a large lingerie advertisement plastered above the plastic seats behind them but the two women were far more entertaining than a provocatively dressed girl. The pretty girl glared while the two women stirred the heart.

Another day was spent on a mission to buy supplies for an art project. Loaded up at the art store I realized there were too many items to carry home without assistance. I was told the store was close by, but it wasn't. Prague may occupy its own culture, yet no matter where I find myself in need of directions, no matter where I find myself lost on foot, the answer is always the same, "It's just a ten-minute walk." My potential saviors always utter this with such blithe confidence, yet it's never a ten-minute walk. I stood outside the store with a couple of large canvases underneath my arms and paint supplies dangling from several small bags knowing the journey home would be tricky, if not impossible. There wasn't a taxi rank in sight.

Then a young student arrived out of nowhere and said, "Here, let me help you."

I lived an hour away and replied, "Really, don't bother, you're too kind, but no."

She gently removed the canvases from underneath my arms. "My boyfriend won't be out of class for another hour or so, I have time."

We walked home and she came in for tea and a talk. I

listened to her politics and to her life and thought she just might change the world.

A couple of days later I was eating lunch at a local neighborhood restaurant. The eatery probably aimed for an upscale clientele but two young locals had another idea. They must be around thirty, both leaning against the railing surrounding the outdoor seating area. They are getting drunk and they've been going at it for a very long time, probably from the night before. The waitress rolls her eyes when walking by with plates for patrons seated outside. The young people laugh while the older men cast weary eyes their way. The rest of the patrons just ignore the two old friends. They are each holding a large bottle of beer, challenging one another, threatening to come to blows if the other doesn't rise to the occasion and continue their game. Sometimes one of them teeters, accompanied by a long, loud belch, and falls. After a few minutes he gets back up and the game continues. I could blame it on the moon as some people do. Instead, I'm pretty convinced these Slavs occupy their own society, slightly distant, and most of the time, kind.

WHEN THE WEATHER warmed up I was on the bus, and within twenty minutes, swimming laps at my new pool. The pool in Paris had been indoors and small, with delicately painted tiles beneath the water, and periwinkle blue lighting above to keep the Parisien swimmers relaxed. The pool in Prague was Olympic sized, outside and located in the neighborhood called *Praha 4*. It had plenty of lanes to swim continuously without hassle. After forty minutes my reward came in the form of a long steam bath. A sauna is therapeutic but nothing can compete with a steam bath because it feels like a luxury, where I can silently inspect the young women with their long lines and flat stomachs. Shaving pubic hair may be trendy but here they have plenty of hold outs.

The conversations continued whether fully clothed or nude, like the rest of Europe, no one was self-conscious except for me. Unlike the rest of Europe, where older French women pride themselves on staying razor thin, and Italian women make an attempt, here, the older women happily let their bodies go. They resemble large buddha goddesses before disappearing behind the steam. They are serene and completely oblivious seated on either side as my body relaxes through osmosis.

Early on, I met two women to talk with on a regular basis. One, named Gabrielle owned a flower store and I am a good client. She's also a well known local singer who performs arthouse techno in local clubs. Gabrielle is lovely. Another woman, named Jan owns a music store with a wonderful DVD selection, where I can rent movies from the past. Gabrielle is Moravian, Jan is Bohemian. Each well versed in their own history. I can sense the divide and it is subtle. It channeled a former conversation with a female friend from Berlin whose parents spoke of East Germany as if it still existed. History is never forgotten here, it still hurts and can linger in the ether for her citizens.

There are plenty of expats and they are completely immersed in their host country. Every single one of the Americans I met spoke fluent Czech, along with a Russian woman named Lola. She was special, and became a good friend and did resemble a showgirl. Lola was gorgeous, with light blonde hair and delicate features. She was well educated and heavily engaged with the burgeoning new

political party called "The Pirate Party". Francis took
interest and followed the Pirate movement, updating me on
a regular basis. He was convinced they were on the side of
the angels. A lot of engineers made up this progressive political party and they were getting mobilized throughout
Europe and beyond. They were doing well, specifically, in
both Germany and Iceland. Along my travels I met some
key players, just because I asked, and because they were
open to dialogue and serious with their political intentions.

Prague was to play host to an international conference
and Francis suggested we throw them a party. Unfortunately
Francis had to shuttle back to Kazakhstan before the conference even began. I had met Rick Falkvinge two years earlier;
he was the guy responsible for starting the political party in
the first place. Rick was a truly unique character from
Sweden who made himself available through conferences
and twitter. If you sent a tweet, he replied, and when I was in
the same city, we met for a beer, once in Berlin, another time
in Amsterdam. My casual acquaintance with Rick became a
running joke because Francis was the one who wanted to
meet him but his schedule always got in the way. Being a
dilettante I followed the party because it was a unique political trend making a dent in European politics. If I wasn't
serious about their cause I appreciated a reason to throw a
party.

I enlisted Lola; she was always keen and generous in
spirit. Once she came over and spent hours teaching me
how to make Borscht; it was a fantastic dinner for three.
Another time her mother flew in from St. Petersburg and I
had them over for dinner. The more I asked about Putin the
more mysterious he became, as if waters run deep with
Russians, as if they internalize an entirely separate sense of
time. But I did try, but often heard Russians prefer to act as a

collective group of souls, as much as I herald from the land of the individual. Lola's mother was lovely and more weary than any Roman I ever met.

I prepared for the Pirate Party based on nothing but hope. I bought several cases of Italian wine and Pilsner beer and made plenty of finger food and waited. I attended the conference but there was no way of knowing who might show up. No fewer than fifty guests stopped by our apartment on the last night of the conference representing well over a dozen countries. The Pirate Party had a silly name but they were becoming the fastest growing political party in Europe. The German arm was growing more sophisticated by expanding their platform beyond its focus on copyright and internet freedoms. In Germany their manifesto now included childcare, wages, and other issues important to any society.

I tuned into my bohemian ideals and opened my joint to a bunch of strangers. It was my best fete ever. The party was mellifluous with every guest engaged with everyone else even if they wondered who the hell I was. Not that anyone cared because they were just happy to argue about everything in good spirit. The German and Dutch journalists debated with the Pirate members, the English came across as slightly cynical and opportunistic, and when the Italian journalists arrived they asked to see the wine selection. It was comforting to know cultural realities are alive and well at Chez Bay. The party kept going and lasted until the early morning hours and it was quite possibly the highlight of my year.

*...civilized destinations*

OUR FINANCES WERE flush and travel and rental cars were on
the menu again. Salzburg had always been a destination for
various reasons; Francis trusted their banks and his parents
had lived nearby in Bad Reichenhall for many years. Vienna
was a destination because it had all the art in the world. It
was where I could stand in line and hear the Viennese
whisper "Klimt and Schiele," in the same way they whis-
pered Mozart. There was opera and music and I ate chocolate cake with my coffee in the morning. I went to Vienna
and Salzburg as often as possible.

Prague was civilized too, it was the kind of place where
we ate ice cream and sipped cognac on a lazy Sunday afternoon in a nearby park, sitting inside a Gazebo, gazing at the
vineyards cascading down the hill. I wasn't wearing a purple
velvet jacket but I did find a place to drink absinthe, to see
what all the fuss was about; which wasn't much. The
essence of Kafka was everywhere, and now I understood
how this city's ancient magnetism had charmed commoners
and kings over the centuries. I also understood why
Bohemia was the sort of creature Franz Kafka once
described as, "A little mother that has claws".

She had sharp edges and soft lines. Prague's expat
community was calm and far less competitive than Paris. I
networked at meetups and met plenty of Bohemians and
Moravians in these eclectic crowds. As a whole the country
kept its distance, at least financially from the EU yet there
was always this great sense of solidarity in the countries in
which I lived and experienced in Europe. They sincerely
tried to get rid of their corrupt politicians, but everyone
does, without much luck. I never thought I'd get a job in
Prague and I was still writing; not getting paid much but

that wasn't the point. And I was starting to write about my travels on a regular basis. I had been keeping a blog since Rome, a random collection of perceptions and was now grateful because there was so much to recall.

∼

*...Boris*

∼

HOWEVER, there was a problem brewing regarding the idiosyncratic family who owned the building we lived in. They were charming at first and then they became a problem. Eventually I realized they probably didn't acquire the building by paying cash, rather their ownership was more likely derived from the State's re-distribution process in the mid 90's. The father and his wife lived downstairs, in the basement, and their daughter and her partner lived directly above our flat.

Initially, the paperwork and process felt familiar until the family started to become a part of my life. This was due to close proximity as well as their peculiar attitude toward fixing fundamental issues like heating and hot water. If I had a large piece of art to hang on my bedroom wall, the father was all too eager to assist. But when the colder months approached the heating began to malfunction. Boris, my landlord, came over with his screwdriver and played with the gizmo on the wall for about an hour, until it started to work and then it began to break once a week. As it broke more often we started to argue each time. It was obvious the pipes needed to be cleaned. I called the real estate agent and she called him and we concluded he didn't want to spend the money. The boiler needed air for the fire to start up but when I suggested I hire a proper technician he became very agitated. I got Francis involved but he just got frustrated. He said, "He's just talking nonsense and he's not going to pay to have it fixed."

Boris was a very nervous guy and his method was to wear us down with nonsensical words, without any of that Italian charm. I noticed he hired one person to come into the building, a young guy that came each week to scrub the stairs. He spent the entire day scrubbing each stair as if this was the most important item on his list. Sometimes I watched the family from my balcony. The mother and daughter worked in the garden and Boris just ran around flapping his arms in a perpetual state of confusion. It came down to the fact that they didn't think the tenant had the right to have heat and hot running water on a regular basis. There was an Indian couple across the corridor and a Turkish couple upstairs I had met a few times, but I didn't feel like investigating because Boris made me feel uncomfortable, and I suspected he might be suffering from dementia.

Francis was spending more time in Romania and said, "Listen, he's not going to have it fixed, he's nuts. But if you want to see more of me you can either move to Bucharest or Almaty, the capital of Kazakhstan."

"I'm not moving to Kazakhstan."

"I wouldn't expect you to," he said. "But Bucharest is interesting, you can watch it boom before your eyes."

Bucharest didn't inspire anything in particular but living with my husband did. It was enough to say good-bye to Central Europe and welcome the opportunity to check out Eastern Europe. We didn't renew our lease and Boris was an asshole. Still, Prague was a treat. I took the overnight train with Colette and Godot to Bucharest, with a stopover in Hungary, met with a couple of realtors, came back to Prague and started the necessary research. Moving countries was starting to resemble something as regular as a trip to the grocery store.

# 30

# BUCHAREST: WHEN TIME INSPIRED THE FUTURE

### 2013

~

T he jury was out regarding the cultural benefits of Bucharest, but our Romanian landlord was a real engineer, as opposed to someone pretending to be one. When something broke or was in need of repair, which was rare, she had it fixed without questions. Our new apartment was spacious and nondescript, affordable and centrally located near Herestrau Park. Our luck with landlords had returned.

It was the most pragmatic move so far. I spent time recruiting as well as locating a larger office for Francis's expanding company. The country was foreign but the company was familiar. Francis recruited software consultants from Seattle and an old colleague from London. Our dinner table was full of faces from the past as well as Romanians, who were Latin and happy to be social. This was in stark contrast to the Kazakhs who remained distant and cagey. Our guests from Eurasia acted like spies and gave nothing away. Their roles at the Romanian office were often mysterious and they kept to themselves, in packs of Kazakhs.

Foreigners came to Kazakhstan for their resources, not for talent, and they were welcomed as long as they arrived with bribes. Expertise wasn't appreciated but money was; at least the Kazakhs didn't boil their foes like their neighbors in Uzbekistan. And there was never any desire to travel with Francis to their land. The furthest east I ventured was to Bulgaria, overnight, to visit the Black Sea. I thought about driving to Turkey, which would have been a treat, then pulled back. I must have known my odyssey was finally beginning to wind down.

The Kazakhs killed off any curiosity being walled off socially, and eventually they would test Francis and his ethics, but the Romanians did not. These people were anxious to compete on the world stage although there was a specific dividing line between generations. If I met a Romanian over forty it was evident they were still softly tied to their communist past. The younger ones were eager to shed previous politicians and bad policies. They wanted food on the shelves and a future to include working in the private sector. They wanted to make it on their own. With affection I referred to them as the 'Romaniacs'.

*...the Romaniacs*

~

AN ARGUMENT COULD BE MADE that Romania proved more savvy regarding technology than most European countries. If they had further to go by the time I arrived in 2012 they were shifting into fourth gear. The Romanian government had intentionally produced a disproportionate amount of engineers by incentivizing them with tax cuts. In the 70's they experimented with higher degrees and institutional programs. Then the State government specifically created an attractive new reality by giving engineers a large tax break in the early 2000's. Companies paid taxes but individuals were allowed exemption. What the Romaniacs lacked in their ecosystem they made up in sheer gung-ho attitude.

It reminded me of Seattle in the mid 90's, with the exception they were Latin, and could exhibit a loose grip on the concept of process. One of the Romaniacs I met had managed to secure a long-term IT project in Germany.

When he came to dinner I asked about his progress. "The engineers I've placed on the project aren't so impressed by the Germans," he said casually. Three months later I ran into him and asked for an update. His relaxed attitude had changed, "It is more difficult than we thought, I guess there is something to the German engineer."

What was known to Francis early on was Romania's ability to produce a large number of smart engineers, certainly more than any other country in the EU. Silicon Valley and Seattle companies started outsourcing their business at college towns like Iasi, (pronounced 'yesh') and Romania became the number one place for outsourcing engineers in Europe.

Francis was spot on prior to our move. Modernity unfolded in the form of skyscrapers lining up against the sky and the roads were often in better condition than those in Italy. Romanian roads had been notoriously poor for decades, without critical highways, yet I experienced the benefits of the European Union on a daily basis. Whenever I drove through Romania or the Czech Republic there were giant signs of the EU flag along the roads, proudly adver-

tising their contribution to new and improved
infrastructure. This allowed great change and expansion for
its citizens.

The first six months in Bucharest were spent immersing
myself in their world. I got to know them through work and
was invited to a wedding where I danced the traditional
*Hora*. I wasn't fussed when getting dressed, and pulled out a
long, black clingy skirt from my closet. I wondered why I
hadn't worn it for such a long time and was reminded while
dancing the *Hora*. Each time we closed in on the circle
everyone lifted their hands high above their head, and each
time my skirt started to fall down. I think one or two women
were suspicious of my wardrobe choice which I found
funny. Flirting with a Romanian was never on my bucket
list.

The Romaniacs I met yearned to reverse the disdain
received in the past. They wanted to earn the kind of respect
German, and more specifically American engineers
garnered. It was exciting to watch the change in real time. I
could feel the energy and desire, and the Romaniacs had a
major advantage specific to the internet: they spoke English.
Many of them carried Roman names like Remus and
Marius. Their history was diverse with distinct ties to a
distant Rome. When it was part of Austria the Italians
wanted to remind the Romanians they were their 'cousins'
so Mussolini sent a bronze statue of the Capitoline wolf to
several cities in Romania. Underneath the statue was written; "ai suoi figli sperduti, da roma madre" "to her lost children, from mother Rome".

The Capitoline Wolf is used in both Romania and
Moldova as a symbol of their Latin origin, perhaps due to
being geographically surrounded by Slavs. The statues lived
proudly in a couple of cities I drove through and there were

an awful lot of guys named Florin, Dorin, or Sorin. Over dinner one night all three sat at our table eating my petit di pollo alla Milanese. I asked Sorin about the gypsies and he used an anecdote from his personal experience to explain the Roma culture.

"When I was at University," he said, "I made a deal with my dad, if I got straight A's he should buy me a computer. I got straight A's but he didn't get me a computer so I ran away. When we were at school the gypsies attended class until they turned eleven or twelve years old. That's when their parents took them out of school and put them into their own culture. When I ran away I remembered my best friend at school. Ten years later he was a gypsy but he never forgot our friendship and let me stay with his family. They are loyal. They might steal, but they are loyal friends, even if they haven't seen them for a long time."

I asked, "Did your father ever get you a computer?"

"No, he didn't, but I'm an IT manager in a major company." Francis was instrumental in building that company and that's probably why he shared the story. Francis had high regard for the Romanians and he believed in their talent, they in turn stayed loyal to Francis, at least the younger ones did. One of the older ones, whom Francis had flown in from Seattle, resorted to his country's old ways and caused major problems for Francis; thankfully, he was not a part of my story.

But I found Sorin's story instructive in the same way I found the homes on the outskirts of Bucharest educational in a cultural way. They were built with 'dirty money' as it was called. These homes, or structures were illustrative of the origin of the Roma gypsies. I encountered them en route to Austria or on my way to tour the Carpathian Mountains by car. They stood separate from the rest. Their facade was exotic and appeared out of nowhere as if I had suddenly landed in India. One could argue these structures told the story of their migration from India over 300 years ago. The Roma spoke their own language and they had their own rules. If I slowed down to get a better look at one of these buildings, invariably, a group of gypsies would approach my slow moving car and suggest it was time to move along, and fast.

I was tricked by the gypsies in the city more than once. If I saw a young woman in a wheelchair with a blanket strategically placed over her lap, making it appear she didn't have any legs; I bought it. She'd compete for my attention mimicking the universal sign for smoking a cigarette so I bought her a pack of cigarettes. The following day the same young woman was running around on both legs, each in fine shape, hands outstretched for handouts. When she caught my eye she started laughing and I had to join her. She was harmless compared to the gypsies who came up to my car warning me to drive away.

Their religion was harder to figure out. It was Eastern Orthodox, managed by the Metropolitan, although some seemed to consider themselves more Roman Catholic than the Italians. It could be confusing regarding their ancient history with Constantinople and I enjoyed visiting a small Orthodox Church called Biserica Kretzulescu. It sat on the side of a major boulevard downtown called Calea Victoriei. Inside, the pews surrounded the main space, rather than lining up in the middle, and it created a uniquely serene atmosphere for their protocol and prayer.

# 31

## ANOTHER PEACEFUL PILGRIMAGE

~

It was at this time that Colette started having seizures. She was now fifteen years old and her Venetian face was turning grey. Colette had been with me every step of the way throughout my odyssey. She died on Good Friday and it broke my heart.

Muv used to stare at her and say, "I just think she's too perfect to paint." It was easy to meditate on Colette. The first day I brought her home I was told to keep her in the kennel at night. I lay on my side and we stared at one another until I took her out and put her on my bed. For the next fifteen years she slept on a little pillow above my head. She watched my every move whenever we were in the same room.

When Francis and I got married we decided to get a dog. After Colette we decided to get two; Godot came along the following year. My research took me to a breeder in Vancouver, Washington, located about three hours south of Seattle. I discovered later on this was the same small town where my biological daughter, Heidi, was adopted by the preacher and his wife. This wasn't the only coincidence; Colette weighed the same as my daughter did at birth; four pounds nine ounces. I didn't know it then but the moment I saw Colette peaking out from behind the couch, looking so shy, perhaps abused as a puppy, I knew she was the one.

In her final week she went both blind and deaf. As with Muv, everything happened very quickly, for which I was grateful. That didn't stop her from slipping outside her little round bed to sniff me out until she found me at my desk. Colette had followed my entire life with her eyes and her heart, but then she stopped eating. Neither of us wanted to experience another grand seizure. She was telling me it was time to go. The Romanian vet came to our house and she died quietly in my arms.

Francis and I drove out to the countryside to find the perfect spot for such a special little creature. We drove around windy roads and astounding views. We passed dozens of little wooden churches, resembling petite A-frames, strewn across the mountain roads. Each of these was ridden with religious icons tucked inside their tiny 'churches' called Troita's. Whenever a faithful Romanian passed a Troita they instantly made the sign of the cross in midair. This made me smile knowing Colette would receive prayers throughout the day. We buried her in a place with a beautiful view overlooking Lake Vidraru in the shadow of the Fagaras mountains. There was a waterfall nearby, it was peaceful and perfectly suited for the unbearable lightness of being Colette. In the end she weighed next to nothing and we could easily imagine her floating up to the stars. Colette could do her pirouettes and entertain them with a face like a Venetian mask, a face far too pretty to paint.

When I let her go it felt like a sign to set off on another

pilgrimage. We had driven through Transylvania and cruised through the Carpathian Mountains, so the time was ripe for another kind of pilgrimage, taken by car. I can't recall if it was Florin, Dorin, or Sorin, but one of them told me about two mountain roads situated between the highest peaks in the country. Two highly atmospheric roads rarely open to the public. One of the barely paved roads is called "Transfagarasan" and the other is called the "Transalpina".

The car show, "Top Gear," drove their Ferraris along this crazy maze and giggled the entire time. These two roads created a strange labyrinth of spiraling roads without railings, a roller coaster of a trip, making the driver giggle or feel like he was driving at the edge of the earth. They sat along the southern section of the Carpathian Mountains, and were constructed in the 70's, during the reign of Nicolae Ceausescu. He wanted to ensure a quick military access across the mountains in case of a Soviet invasion. They weren't the only roads, but these passes took the driver through river valleys creating a highly dramatic tour. When viewed from the air these roads appeared almost as bizarre and disorienting as when driving right on top of them. They are windy, dotted with steep hairpin turns, long S-curves, and sharp descents.

I got an old rental car, put Godot in the passenger seat, and felt confident for no other reason than Godot had arrived and Colette was now gone. Estimated time was under three hours for each road. I made a reservation to stay overnight in Sibiu, a town with a German mayor, situated in between the two roads, assuming a break would be necessary.

For long stretches I never saw another car. Then I noticed a cluster of shacks in the trees with a more modern building located closer to the road, with bold letters at least three feet high streaked across the front, "TESSERA ALEX". Alexandru was a common name in this country but I read it as if Muv had come along for the ride and that felt wonderful. It was an unforgettable experience because the isolating effect was surreal and the scenery spectacular. It was the kind of pilgrimage that would inspire the future.

# 32

# TIME FOR A DRAMATIC DECISION

∼

W hen I got back to the flat I received a call from the government letting me know my residency card was ready to be picked up. It took six months, and to my surprise, it took that amount of time to ask the most obvious question of all, "How in the hell did I end up in Bucharest?"

I hadn't even considered the question until the guy at the Ministry of Foreign Affairs did. I stared at his youthful face beneath a shock of black hair, a face full of honest confusion, as he slid my new residency card beneath the glass. He shook his head, utterly perplexed and said, "You're an American, why would you move here?"

I didn't have a short answer because I never did, so I cast my palms towards the sky and thanked him with a smile. I put my glossy new Bucharest Residency ID card in my purse and walked out. There were more questions to ask myself. Were we heading in the wrong direction? Had our peripatetic lifestyle taken on a life of its own and gone rogue?

These were valid concerns, if easy to overlook, because I was grateful to have my paperwork in order. Obtaining a new residency card was rarely a simple task, except in Amsterdam, but I wasn't sure life as a gypsy was the right life for me. It wasn't as if I was suffering delusions of being mistaken for a local one but still, I had become an upscale gypsy, the kind that obeys the law.

There wasn't a cafe culture in Bucharest but I found a place to sit down and have a think over a cup of coffee. The majority of moves had been initiated by me as if Francis' nomadic tendencies had become contagious. For him, the rhythm of diverse cultural realities proved a natural extension, enabling him to assimilate with relative ease. But not I. As a child we moved just once, from Napa Valley to Seattle, when I was only two years old and didn't even remember doing it. Now the multiple moves kept knocking me off balance. I suspected there were few moves left and I was tired of drifting. I finished my latte and retraced my steps to the Ministerial building to catch a taxi. As my eyes took in the building I decided it looked a bit dingy, and I contemplated whether the locals perceived it in this way. I knew the answer and the reality of living in Bucharest hit me as hard as the blunt sun beating down on the city's eclectic combination of modern, medieval and communist architecture. It was time to make a dramatic decision.

When I got home I wandered over to the living room window and stepped out onto the small balcony overlooking the busy street. I watched how they drove back and forth below, noting how little they observed the white lines or signs of any kind. They honked constantly. As if playing out my own silent revolt to their erratic and random ways I began to write about why I left Seattle in the first place. I was about to turn fifty and Francis was happily building his little empire but my part-time job had come to a close. I was feeling slightly idle which is an ideal time to write. I had started writing travel essays in Prague but I needed to get honest about the choices I'd made and why I left the States in the first place.

Gazing into my rear-view mirror it was easy to ascertain which dates proved significant in shaping the initial stages of my odyssey. How that first domino was pushed by Muv, and then the events leading up to the Transatlantic voyage, yet the rest of the moves had been primarily initiated by me. My odyssey was arriving at its final chapter.

The concept of time was subtle in Bucharest and then it started to feel like it had flipped backwards. The East was gaining liberties while the West appeared to be losing them. Gore Vidal had been writing about this for decades and I started to read his essays more seriously since Lignano. I watched Eastern Europeans embrace their new freedoms in the same way I had once needed to become financially dependent in Seattle. During that time there was the freedom to build a business without feeling like I was being watched the entire time, and long before that, when I could hop a plane a half hour before departure when I was ten years old. The latter wouldn't happen here, or anywhere because the surveillance economy was on its way. I needed to find a new kind of future and I needed to make a dramatic decision.

I was awfully tired of living in rentals in the middle of the city. I felt little need to acquire more friends, and rely on materialistic tendencies. I wanted to experience something new, outside of city life. If the first half of my life was devoted to making stuff happen, the next phase was to review why it happened in the first place. I would need to find a quiet place to reflect.

My host country was careening into its own future with a frenzy. However, the Romanians I met were always saving up for a little place in the country, where they could take advantage of their rich soil and grow their own gardens. The hustlers thrived in the city, but the Romanians loved their countryside and wide open spaces in a particularly sentimental way. Their old folktales remained active within their collective imagination. But they weren't mine.

Whenever Francis and I drove outside the city, we'd pass by little old women sitting on their rickety wooden benches by the side of the road, maybe a box of fruit for sale at their feet. We'd catch their scrunched up faces, heavily wrinkled, without a day of moisturizer, making Francis nostalgic, "Look at her, she could be my grandmother, and just look at the soil. Italian soil was black and rich like that not too long ago."

My odyssey often felt like an exercise in trying to catch the last gasp of old world charm. This is what I was thinking as we drove by the old homes, and that's when I knew Italy was the solution. However, I wanted to enjoy the parts of Italy that remained untouched, and authentic. In particular, I thought about the part of Italy where I received my first proper introduction, long before Lake Garda and Rome.

# 33

# PIEMONTE

~

As a tourist, I was familiar with Italy's grand cities and monuments, but once I met Francis, and whenever we visited his family's place in Limone, in Piemonte, I began to experience it through his eyes. This was when the country's mentality opened up and became known to me. This region, located in northwest Italy, intuitively felt like such a solid place, and Francis was quite keen on the idea. He considered Limone to be the center of the universe. A sentimental town where family weddings and funerals took place. And I agreed, it had charm but it was a mountain village, nestled on the border to France. It was a place to go skiing and that wasn't my style.

The idea took time to formulate as I began taking several trips from Bucharest to Piemonte. The search became extensive due to the fact it could result in the most important decision of our lives. I was immediately drawn to those homes in the wine country because I was born into that culture, in Napa Valley, therefore it made sense to end up amongst the vines. My idea gained traction because it felt simultaneously pragmatic and romantic. There was no desire to buy a vineyard and we didn't have that much money, but we could buy a lot of land because there was plenty of it in Piemonte. The realtor showed me homes in the provinces of Asti and Cuneo. Being married to an engineer inspired me to perceive his kind of expertise as living alongside the farmers because both contributed to our future, both created things people needed. The dream was accompanied with a bonus; the farmers could teach me how to create and grow my own garden.

This notion of becoming self-sufficient had simmered in my subconscious for quite awhile. I had listened to people talk about this concept in the same way sailors discussed cruising offshore, but rarely did. Every home I was shown came with their own version of a garden, and even if I wasn't entirely sure what I was looking for I was getting older and knew that I wanted to be surrounded by nature. As if this could assist with aging gracefully, and I could learn about herbs and their healing powers. I could grow my own flowers instead of spending so much money on them, and if climate was creating havoc I wanted to be where it was causing the least amount. Being surrounded by the Alps simply felt like an extra benefit. I remembered how solid they felt while living in Geneva and now I could be surrounded by several, including Italian, Swiss and French mountains bordering the region of Piemonte.

Italy's success at exporting their culture was heightened with the majority of its products coming from our next home. Piemontese farmers produced rice for the rest of Europe, and the Swiss came here to make their chocolate because of the prized hazelnuts, not to mention the truffles, the world famous wine, award winning cheese and so much more.

With each excursion to Italy the idea expanded in my mind as if I really could save the tiniest piece of the planet by saving myself and growing some of my own food. Food was being further removed from the consumer and I wanted to reverse the trend. And I really wanted to learn how to listen to the trees, if only to better to understand myself and explore that idea of embracing some grace. A life of contemplation wasn't just a fanciful idea—it became a goal to achieve; and it weren't for my short life as a live-aboard in Lignano I doubt I could have craved nature with such a growing intensity. That time spent in Venice, when we were broke, was probably the best investment ever made.

And the very moment I saw our future home it offered the same impact experienced while walking across the Tiber River into the neighborhood of Trastevere; Italy was no longer limited to acting as a balm, if offered a new frontier, and I was ready for the future.

## 34

# WHEN TIME FELT SPIRITUAL

*...one year later*

❧

Oscar Wilde once said, "There are two tragedies in life, one is not getting what you want, the other is getting it".

I hadn't traveled this far just for a home; I was going to make it a paradise. The work required was far more than imagined and the rewards were immense. There was a lot of land for future vines and hazelnuts trees but the focus remained on our immediate surroundings. There were basics to maintain and there was an Arcadia to create. Everything exceeded expectations. If I wanted four seasons our new home came with no less than a dozen. There was a specific calendar for planting the vegetables and cherry trees in spring, cutting back the roses in February, fertilizing the lawn in the fall, stocking the wood in early spring, and collecting apples, pears and baby plums from the orchard in late summer.

At the height of summer the fireflies arrived to create their white magic at night. When it was time for the vendemmia I helped my neighbors harvest grapes in the morning and learned about the vines that created the wine I loved to drink at night.

There were multiple tasks and I could barely keep up. The water filters in our well needed to stay clean and I had to make sure our gas tank carried adequate supply, and didn't have any leaks. When we suspected a leak the gas repair guy arrived and lit his Bic lighter below the attachment to the house, letting me know we had a leak. He fixed it and I never checked it again.

In spring the shutters flew open and the majority of time was spent planting several types of lettuce and tomatoes, green beans, strawberries, potatoes and finocchio. I planted dozens of roses in the ground in every available space and let the sundavilles and colorful annuals spill out of all the vases surrounding the patio and the pool. The more I planted the more I had to weed yet I couldn't stop myself. We moved in during the month of May and by mid-summer we had a garden that could feed us for months. Each month a new blossom arrived and I couldn't believe our good fortune. I planted hundreds of saffron bulbs I'd bought from Sardinia and by October I had enough to fill a large jar. The quality of what I could produce never ceased to amaze and all it took was time, and patience.

It was the kind of work I grew to love. A large lawn surrounded the house, demanding my attention, and the smaller tiles around the pool required maintenance if they weren't properly covered in winter. I placed a white statue of a goddess at each corner of the pool for dramatic effect, giving them names like Colette, Persephone, Penelope and

Alexandria. They required no work because they were perfect.

It took over two hours to mow the lawn which had to be completed twice a week in summer and I loved every minute. If the Piemontese didn't take their lawn seriously, as an American, I did. The lawn was like a metaphor, it taught me how to edit better, and the jungle of weeds fighting helped decipher which battles to choose in life.

I opened the pool in May and didn't cover it til late October. It was tricky to maintain and if the heat increased too quickly the water could turn green so I monitored the pool's temperature every morning. Swimming laps was a luxury and all I had to do was walk out the back door.

Francis was elated by our choice but still traveled, that would never change, which meant I had to do all the work. Sometimes I brought in a gardener to assist with large projects but they were always difficult to find when you live in the middle of nowhere. Our well, our 'pozzo', remained a mystery at first because I never knew how long the water would last. The irrigation system was elaborate and I often worried we might run out of water, but we never did, the water went down over a 100 meters into the ground. The Piemontese know how to prepare for droughts and extreme weather.

The gas tank heated the radiators, which was great, but it was expensive. When the broiler broke I found a technician to install a new one. He did it quickly and efficiently and kept a cigarette dangling from his mouth the entire time. I kept checking on him and walking out of the house in case it blew up. The Piemontese are a tough tribe and feel no fear, if they have any it's reserved for the government.

In the autumn I began using our fireplace and by early winter I kept the fire going all day long. It was an elaborate stone structure with a large glass door and air valves funneling warm air throughout the lower story. This was clever because our home wasn't built in classic Piemontese style with multiple rooms. The lower story was one, long, spacious room with windows extending across the front of the house to optimize the view.

It must have been the view that made us fall in love with our new home. The lawn extended out to a border full of heather and below the heather a large vineyard cascaded down the hill full of Moscato and Dolcetto grapes. Beyond our lawn, beyond the heather, and into the distance sat the Ligurian alps to one side and Savona on the other. The mountain view dropped in the middle creating a V-shape, the effect making it appear as if this was the chalice I had been looking for all along. The neighbors owned the vineyard and beyond the vines sat our tiny hamlet called Loazzolo. It was over 1500 years old and boasted the smallest DOC in all of Italy. The wine was fantastic and our tiny town might as well have been New York because that was all the company I craved.

When hunting season began the men would congregate in the 'casetta', a small stone building at the bottom of our private road. After a successful day of killing wild boar the hunters would meet, eat Bolitto con Osso and drink Barolo wine and sometimes I was invited if they caught me driving by on my way home. They seemed so happy or perhaps I was just happier than I'd even been. Whenever I asked a question and they wanted to me understand, they'd stray away from their Piemontese, Loazzoleze, or Bubbiese dialect and speak Italian. I heard them tell tales they must have been telling one another for years. They led a simple life, had few expectations and found me easy to tease.

The vineyards were an ideal barometer for each season.

They showed great promise with their tiny buds in spring and by early summer their leaves were long, lush and deeply green. Once the grapes were cut, and carefully taken away by trucks winding their way down the roads, the leaves turned color and exploded in bright orange and yellow; they glistened like jewels in the late autumn. Then, they fell off gradually until the snow came to cover them, leaving them dormant to wait patiently for their owners to visit and trim down their branches until spring arrived and the cycle began all over again. The Italians like to say 'wine is love', and now I believe them.

The house was relatively new but that didn't stop everything from breaking during the first year. The lawn mower broke constantly and if it wasn't the spark plug, I just took a guess, or let it rest and it always started again. Unfortunately, our town was too small for supplies of any kind yet we were blessed with neighbors who shared the long and windy private road that took us to our home on top of the hill. When winter arrived and the snow fell, our neighbor, Alberto, arrived each day at 5am. I heard his tractor arrive on time, driving through our front gate, which I left open so he could enter. I watched him shovel the deep snow away from our garage and clear the large forecourt, only to turn around and drive back down, plowing the snow all the way down to the main road.

The neighbors always helped when necessary and the farmers taught me everything I needed to know about my land. I went on herbal walks with my friend Anna Fila Robbatino who had spent an entire lifetime learning about herbs and happily shared her knowledge on our long nature hikes. Herbs were everywhere in Piemonte, and this region is also known for its magic. The Masca, the witches still roam the forests with their healing powers, and they still gather their knowledge in the same way Anna educated me on our hikes. The soil is toiled well and remains strong to enable the herbs and plants to flourish, allowing Italy to surpass France in both quality and quantity regarding their precious and competitive wine industry.

Piemonte is also known for its nebbia, its thick fog, which lends to the robust grapes producing the fine wines of Barolo, Barbaresco and Barbera. It created a gothic atmosphere as it wound around lyrical hills separating the tiny medieval villages, each with its own fortress on top. Time unfolded slowly in this part of the world. Each village remained separate in dialect and skill sets, each village proud of its own fine cheese, chairs, salami, hazelnuts along with a host of other treasures in a country full of artisans.

If I wanted to be closer to the cycles of life and death and learn how to listen to the trees I found my nirvana. I grew my own herbs and created my own elixir from the ground. I helped to eliminate the space between my vegetables and my dinner table. My new address provided me with a new frontier and kept me completely engaged. I was immersed in my gardening and various tasks in the same way Muv had once focused on her painting. In the same way she applied purpose to her daily and evening routines, I applied this to my outdoor and indoor pursuits. I learned how to focus for long periods of time and the long winters offered little choice. It was a steep curve to listen to the trees but there was plenty of time to reflect on my odyssey.


*...memories and Muv*


∼

INITIALLY IT WAS hard to wrap my mind around the length of my trip, and why it took so long. It became apparent each city presented a personality with specific traits leading me to Piemonte. Memories of Malta made me appreciate the hard work knowing perseverance was critical. Bucharest reinforced the distance traveled and how important it was to plan for the future. If it weren't for Prague I wouldn't have picked up my pen and felt the freedom to unlock the past in the first place. Prague had acted as a gateway in the same way Lignano had opened me up to the healing powers of nature. Paris had been a series of distractions until it was time to embrace the deep grief after losing someone as precious as Muv.

Seattle was ever present because Piemonte reflected her productive attitude by investing their time in the business and pleasure of food and wine. Seattle had trained me to be entrepreneurial and approach the idea of self-sufficiency with abandon. Even *Madi* was ever present. When September arrived I had dozens of shutters to varnish and relished the task, enhancing the cyclical and rhythmic effect life can provide.

However, Rome stood out and forever remained removed from all the other cities. Rome was the beginning of our European odyssey and I felt compelled to return on a regular basis. She would never change and that's why I couldn't while living in the eternal city. Each visit was a treat, retracing steps taken when Colette and Godot still walked with me, now in spirit, to my secret garden deep in the grounds of Doria Pamphili.

When Muv and I spent a month in Europe after my brother's death, we stayed in Turin for a few days, the capital of Piemonte, in between our drive from Venice to Paris. Muv enjoyed Turin the way she appreciated the value of any city yet it was her long nature walks that meant the most; with binoculars around her neck and a handy book in her bag, she caught her beloved birds in action and reported her findings over a phone call. She would gush, "I saw the most extraordinary bird today, you cannot imagine the colors." I would laugh and accept her enthusiasm without understanding her joy, and now I did. Birds woke me up in the morning and they laid eggs in the shade of my flowers in vases surrounding the house. Birds were everywhere and so was the spirit of Muv.

She started to arrive in my dreams. They were silly but had the same message. She would say something odd like, "It's only a bee sting, dear." As if eliminating all the worry I had when things broke down or an allergic reaction from a wasp sting took me to the hospital. It wasn't just a bee sting and I would never step in a shoe left outside with wasps waiting to sting multiple times, but this was one amongst many lessons to learn.

When we bought the house we also brought a new generation of papillons into our life, two brothers we named Gigi and Gaston. They were puppies and Godot played with them on the lawn but he was growing old and tired. Like Colette he had been with me since Seattle and I was so grateful he made it to our final destination. After six months of living in our new home Godot told me it was time to say good-bye. He was 15 years old and one night he had his first seizure. I was so close to nature I knew he wouldn't last through the night. I told Francis to take Gigi and Gaston into the other bedroom and held Godot as the seizures came and went. He barely whimpered and he passed quietly in the early morning hours. Every day he relaxed underneath the tall tomato vines and kept me company while I spent hours weeding my garden. We buried him next to the garden so he could continue hanging out with me. Like Colette, he would be dearly missed, and I had cut some of Colette's hair when she died and buried this piece of her with Godot in the garden.

Muv was convinced I would find my way by taking the long road out. It was a long ladder that I just had to climb. Like her secret, I took my time until finally, I found Piemonte; another secret that needed to be told. I still have my magic carpet. It kept me company at every address. I reupholstered the couch twice since Seattle, but it's the same one we occupied on that fateful night, once upon a time.

Every so often I lay down on that couch and meditate on Muv, taking in the view and listening to the birds, and when I do; I feel perfectly serene.

# ACKNOWLEDGMENTS

I want to thank my editor, John Knight; he proved invaluable, offering encouragement, forever patient, and very kind.

I also want to thank my husband, Francis; it certainly was a trip. Without him, we could have never made it across the pond. Thankfully, our trip continues, together.

I would be remiss if I didn't mention our precious papillons, Colette and Godot, and Gigi and Gaston.

# ABOUT THE AUTHOR

Bailey Alexander was born in Santa Rosa, California, grew up in Seattle and sailed across the Atlantic in 2002. She proceeded to live a nomadic life in Rome, Paris, Malta, Geneva, Venice, Amsterdam, Prague, Bucharest and then settled down in Piedmont, Italy.

Bailey wants to thank the reader for joining her on this European Odyssey, thankfully, the trip continues...

Bailey Alexander's next book is called, "Piemonte; The secret that needs to be told" It's on its way!

For more information on the author and her work, please visit her website

baileyalexander.com

Made in the USA
Coppell, TX
12 January 2024

27522957R10146